Lake Onamia

Lake Pepin

Lake Sanborn

Lake Washington

Lake Whitney

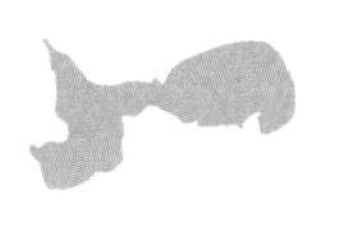

Madison Lake

Marion Lake

Monson Lake

Mud Lake

North Goldsmith Lake

Ogechie Lake

Phelps Lake

Rabbit Lake

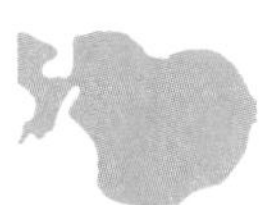

Renneberg Lake

Rice Lake

Ripple Lake

Savidge Lake

Schauer Lake

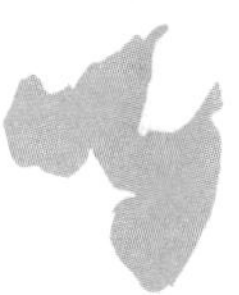

Schilling Lake

School Lake

Section 12 Lake

Section 25 Lake

Severance Lake

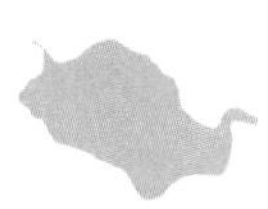

Shakopee Lake

Sheas Lake

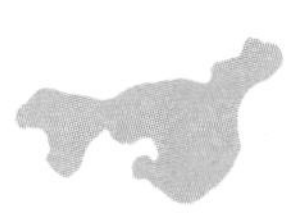

Silver Lake

Spirit Lake

Sweetman Lake

Tamarac Lake

Thomas Lake

Tietz Lake

Turtle Lake

Twenty Lake

Bakers Lake

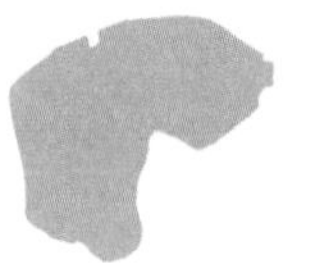

Ballantyne Lake

Barber Lake

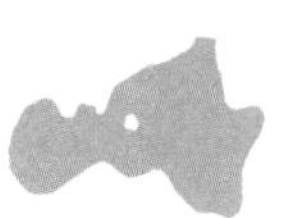

Black Bass Lake

Borer Lake

Clarks Lake

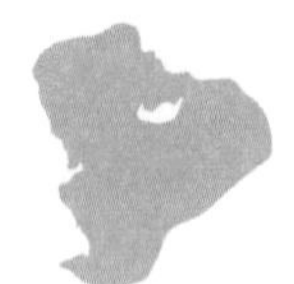

Clear Lake

Curran Lake

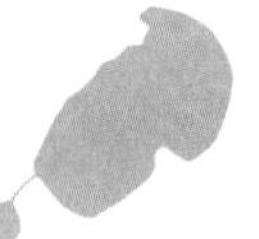

Dam Lake

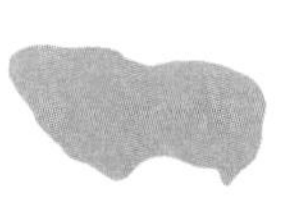

Deer Lake

Dietz Lake

Dog Lake

Duban Lake

Duck Lake

Eagle Lake

Eagle (2) Lake

Eggert Lake

Fadden Lake

Farm Island Lake

George Lake

German Lake

Gilfillin Lake

Goldsmith Lake

Graham Lake

Greenleaf Lake

Hanging Kettle Lake

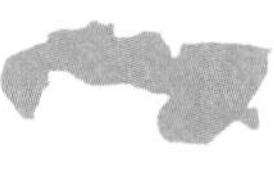

Harkridge Lake

High Island Lake

Johnson Lake

Kings Lake

Lake Addie

Lake Emily

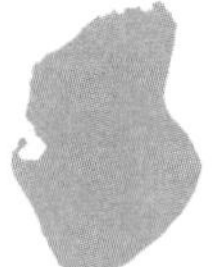

Lake Henry

Lake Jefferson

Lake Mary

With less than 2% of the nation's population, Minnesota is a model for prosperity, creativity, and quality of life.

by Lee Lynch

Designed by Michael Skjei
Cover art by James Keuning

ISBN 13: 978-1-59298-798-6
Library of Congress Catalog Number: 2017908966
Printed in Canada
Second Printing: 2017
21 20 19 18 17   6 5 4 3 2

Beaver's Pond Press, Inc.
7108 Ohms Lane
Edina, MN 55439–2129
(952) 829-8818
www.BeaversPondPress.com

Information contained in this book is primarily from late 2014 to early 2017. Only the top 25 markets were used in any ranking or comparison. Details on many organizations were found on their websites, Facebook pages, and Wikipedia entries.

To order, visit www.ItascaBooks.com or call 1-800-901-3480 ext. 118. Reseller discounts available.

I'm 80, thanks to my internist, **Dr. Michael Cummings**.

I have enough money to pay for this project, thanks to my financial advisor, **John Breon**.

And thanks to my wife, **Terry Saario** *(editor of many drafts), who says, "Enough already."*

Thanks for contributions from:

Walter F. Mondale, former vice president of the United States
R. T. Rybak, Minneapolis Foundation president and former mayor of Minneapolis
Sam Grabarski, former president of the Minneapolis Downtown Council and past executive for the Minnesota State Arts Board
Linda Barrows, poet
Jim Lenfestey, journalist, author, poet

A very special thanks to design genius **Michael Skjei**, who is a cross between Salvador Dali, Milton Glaser, and Charles M. Schulz.

Thanks to **Bonnie Butler Brown** for her ardent pursuit of great photography.

Finally, thanks to **Rosanne Monten**, project manager, whip, wrangler, CFO, and friend.

I was motivated to write this book when my wife, Terry Saario, and I were independently trying to recruit individuals for senior executive positions in the Twin Cities. I was trying to recruit someone from London, and she was hoping to attract a New Yorker. In both cases, they asked for information about life in the Twin Cities.

We thought such information was readily available. Local governments, chambers of commerce, and corporations all had some information, but it tended to be superficial. None conveyed the depth and breadth of how rich life in Minnesota actually is. We then realized that, true to Minnesota's spirit, no one had told the real story of Amazing Minnesota.

I decided to compile a more comprehensive description of life in Minnesota. I began to rank the state and the Twin Cities on almost every dimension of life. How do we compare against other states or localities? What are some unusual facts even locals don't know that would help describe our amazing state?

The more I dug, the more impressed I was by how singular life here is. I became convinced that many Minnesotans and their friends and families would share this wonder about life in this great state.

This book offers hundreds of rankings and facts. Information about many organizations was drawn from their websites, Facebook pages, or Wikipedia entries. I'm certain there are errors as well as omissions, and I hope readers will correct them and add new rankings or factoids at www.amazingmn.com.

My hope is to leave you with a book you would share with family, friends, or someone thinking of leaving or moving to Minnesota. And, of course, you might want to send it to someone who asks, "Why the heck do you live there?"

Lee Lynch

Mn.

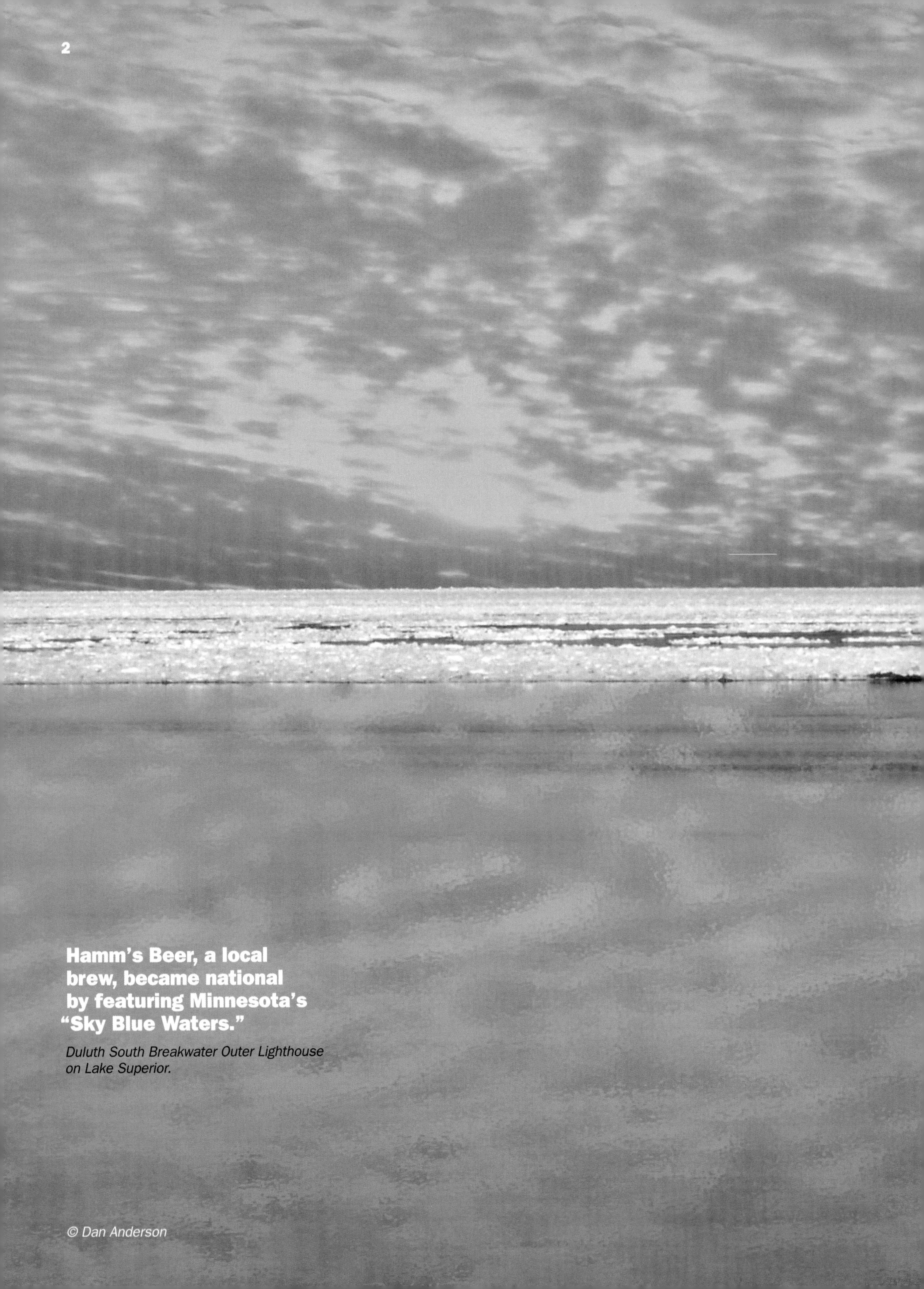

Hamm's Beer, a local brew, became national by featuring Minnesota's "Sky Blue Waters."

Duluth South Breakwater Outer Lighthouse on Lake Superior.

© Dan Anderson

Chapter 1. Stuff you probably know.

The word *Minnesota* comes from the Dakota Sioux name for the Minnesota River, *Mnisota*, which can be translated as "clear blue water." Today there are seven Anishinaabe reservations and four Dakota communities that comprise 1.3% of the state's population.

Public Doman/Photo: Roland Reed/Color: Jared Enos

Spring logjams often needed dynamite to break the jam. Logging then, as it is now, was the nation's most dangerous occupation.

Lumber and milling were the foundations of Minnesota's early industry. Minnesota's rivers were essential to the growth of each. Logs would be floated down the St. Croix, Mississippi, and other rivers to sawmills to meet the demand for lumber in the rapidly growing country.

The Mississippi also provided the power to turn the wheels of flour mills and transportation of these goods to the rest of the nation.

Minnesota by Region

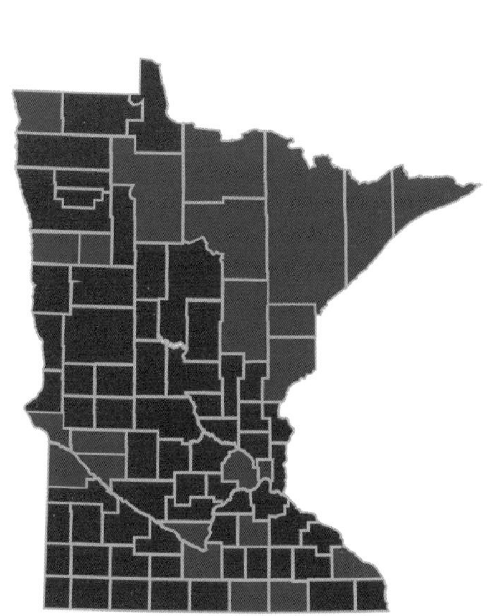

Blue State
Historically, Minnesota has been a "blue" state with an occasional purple tinge. Currently all constitutionally elected state officials are Democrats. The more rural House of Representatives is Republican. Both U.S. senators are Democrats.

Gateway to Canada & North Dakota
Not many people, lots of Native American reservations and snowmobiles.

Rangerville
World's largest open-pit mines, feast or famine, special language *rainch*, not *range*.

Up North
The North Shore of Lake Superior, lots of fresh water, formerly the busiest harbor in U.S., heavy tourism.

Da Cities
Most rich people, most poor people, magnet for both.

Mayochester
Home of the Mayo Clinic, a bunch of colleges, nice mix of Democrats and Republicans.

Wobegon Country
Pretty religious, pretty farms, pretty conservative.

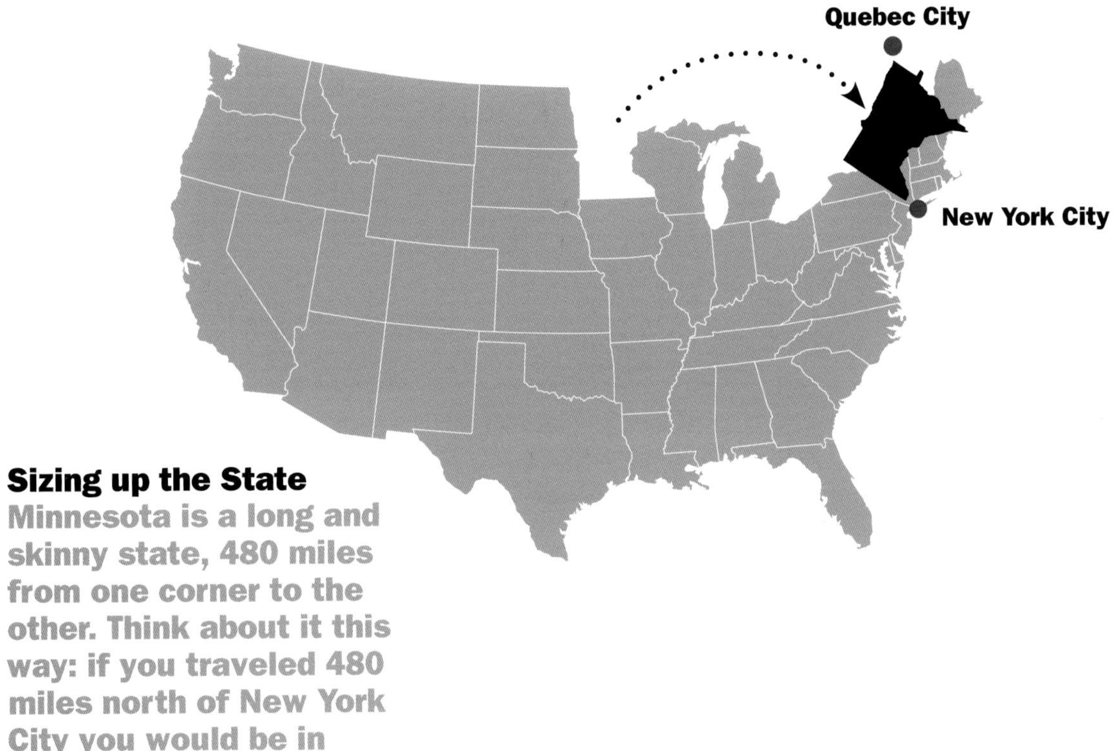

Sizing up the State

Minnesota is a long and skinny state, 480 miles from one corner to the other. Think about it this way: if you traveled 480 miles north of New York City you would be in Quebec City, Canada.

MN
#12&21

Size Comparison

Minnesota is the 12th-largest state in acreage, with a population of 5,489,594, making it the 21st in population.

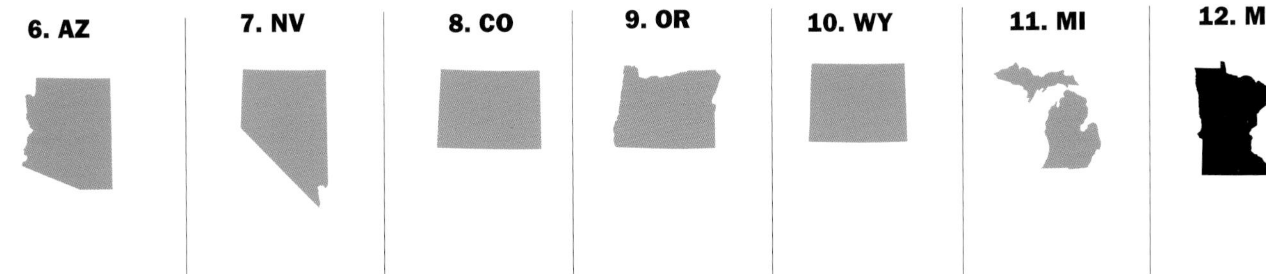

© Steve Lyon

© Joe Mamer Photography/Alamy

To first-time visitors, the cityscape of Minneapolis may seem very small, as does St. Paul. They are only eight miles apart, and together the two cities have a greater metro area population of 3.5 million, making the combination the 17th-largest metropolitan statistical area in the nation.

Minneapolis

The center of finance, theater, entertainment, and restaurants

St. Paul

The city of government, education, and neighborhoods

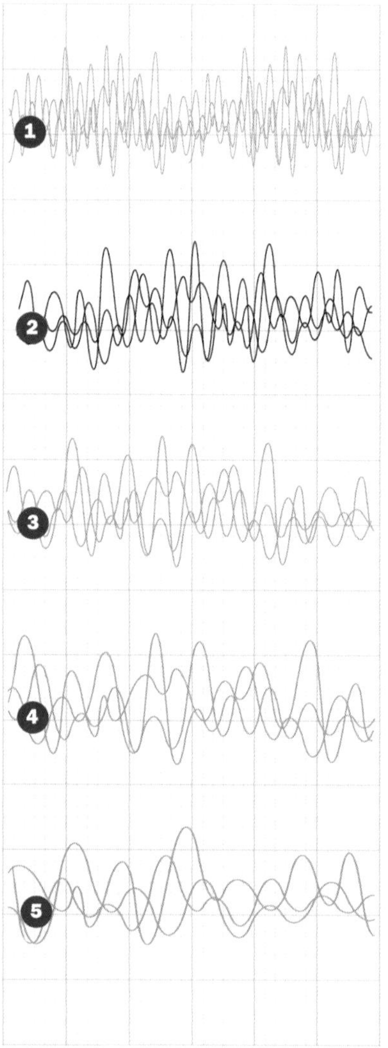

MN
#2

Fastest Talkers

1. Oregon
2. **Minnesota**
3. Massachusetts
4. Kansas
5. Iowa

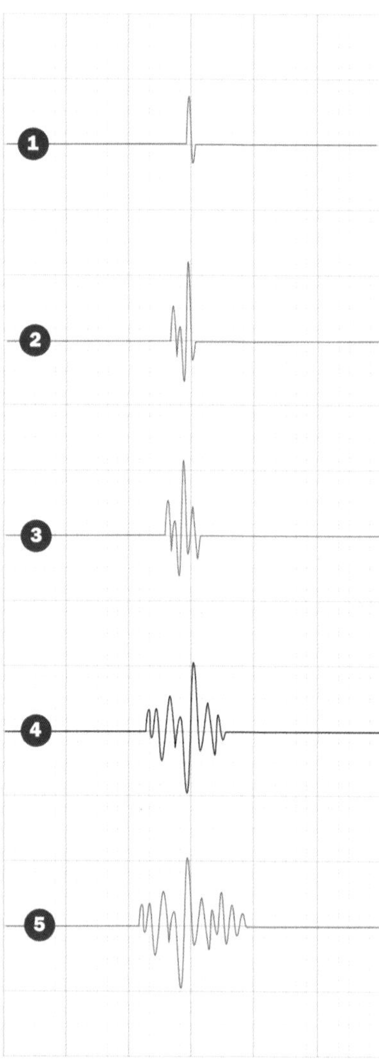

MN
#4

Least Talkers

1. Oklahoma
2. Wisconsin
3. Kansas
4. **Minnesota**
5. Iowa

Minnesotans Don't Talk Much

But when they do, get your hearing aids tuned and prepare to listen. According to the mobile analytics firm Marchex Institute, Minnesotans are the second-fastest-talking folks in the nation.

Oooh ya, I'm from Minnesoooota, but how did ja know?

How to Speak Minnesotan

Minnesota has its own language: "Minnesoooot-an." To speak like a local say the word *Minnesota* slowly, and when you get to the *o* curl your lips like you are going to whistle.

Minnesota has roads everywhere . . . 140,000 miles of them. With only 2% of the nation's population, Minnesota has 6% of its roads. The state's roads and bridges are in better shape than those of the nation.

© Greg Granger

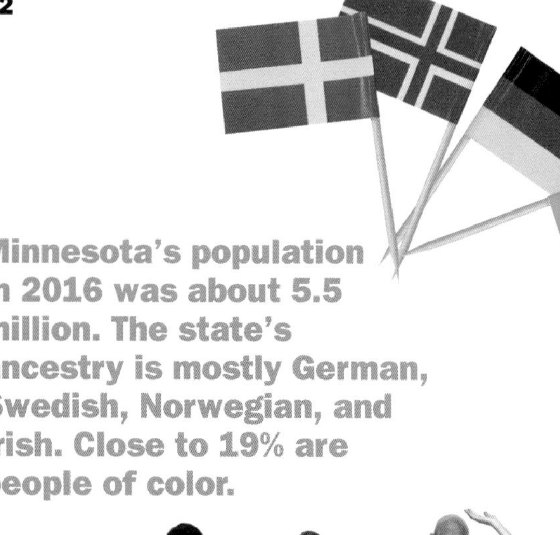

Minnesota's population in 2016 was about 5.5 million. The state's ancestry is mostly German, Swedish, Norwegian, and Irish. Close to 19% are people of color.

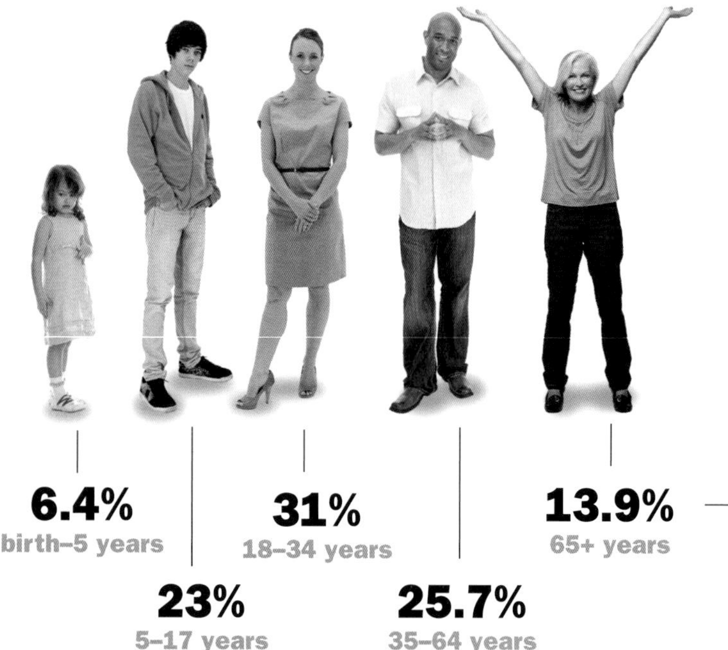

6.4% birth–5 years

23% 5–17 years

31% 18–34 years

25.7% 35–64 years

13.9% 65+ years

MN
#1
$227,700

Home Affordability

Minnesota #1
Atlanta #2

An average home in the Twin Cities costs $227,700.

An average rental apartment in the Twin Cities is $1,042 per month.

The Twin Cities' median household income is $71,008 (2015).

Minnesota's state median income is $63,488 (U.S. average is $56,516).

Millennials Boom

The Millennial population in the Twin Cities has grown by 25% since 2008. *Forbes* and *Atlantic* both rank the Twin Cities among the best for Millennials.

Some Famous Living Native Minnesotans

1. Walter Mondale
2. Bob Dylan
3. Garrison Keillor
4. Jessica Lange
5. Al Franken
6. Jesse Ventura
7. Thomas Friedman
8. Lindsey Vonn

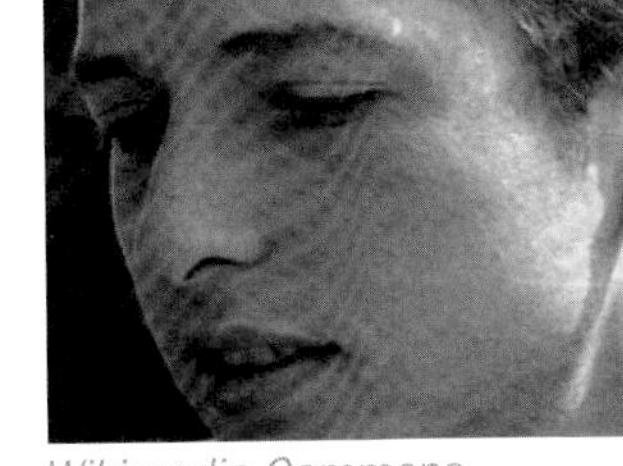

Wikimedia Commons

Wikimedia Commons

© Steven Cohen

Wikimedia Commons

© Steven Cohen

© Steven Cohen

Wikimedia Commons

Wikimedia Commons

Minnesota can get very cold in the winter (you know that) but has world-record-breaking heat in the summer (you didn't know that). Read all about it in the next chapter.

© Make it. MSP

Fat tire biking is the newest winter craze for recreation and commuting. This biker braves heavy snowfall on Lake Harriet in Minneapolis.

© Jim Mone, Associated Press

Chapter 2. Everyone has some stinky days.

Four
Strategies to Deal with Winter.

© Frank Haggerty

Become an expatriate.
Move your family to a warm red state. To deal with those days of extreme heat or high humidity, you will probably stay indoors with the AC on. While many migrate out of Minnesota, consistently low unemployment rates and good jobs attract many to the state.

Hide from winter.
You can wear some of the new high-tech winter gear and cover up or use the 11 miles of skyways in Minneapolis or five miles in St. Paul. The nation's largest indoor mall, the Mall of America with its amusement park and 500 stores, is a great place to hang out in the winter.

MN FACT

Southdale Shopping Center was the first enclosed mall in the U.S., built in 1956 in the Minneapolis suburb Edina.

© Shutterstock

3

Take a sun break.
If it's really cold, damp, or windy, or all three (mega-stinky), it might be a good time for a winter break and a quick trip to someplace warm. Most airlines fly nonstop to dozens of warm spots every day. Thousands of folks leave Minnesota each winter, especially retirees who might spend a couple of months elsewhere. Summer heat brings thousands to Minnesota lakes and the Twin Cities.

4

Embrace winter.
Enjoy the exhilaration and beauty of the season. Dress warm and participate in an array of winter activities and sporting events.

© Sally Hawkins, St. Louis Park, MN

Let's Face It, Minnesota Has Some Stinky Days

Some days you just don't want to take the dog out for a walk. Almost every state has 50 stinky days. A calm, sunny, 20°-above-zero day can be exhilarating, as can a dry 100° day with a light breeze. But a damp, rainy, very cold, or very hot windy day can be "stinky."

MN WTF

62° in February

Future of Weather

January 2017 was the warmest in history for the Twin Cities. A mid-February temperature of 62° surprised everyone.

Snow Shovel Arsenal:

1. The Sacroiliac
2. Norwegian Farmer
3. The Neighbors
4. Back Breaker
5. Slush Pusher
6. The Silicon Valley
7. Da Wife's
8. Screw It!

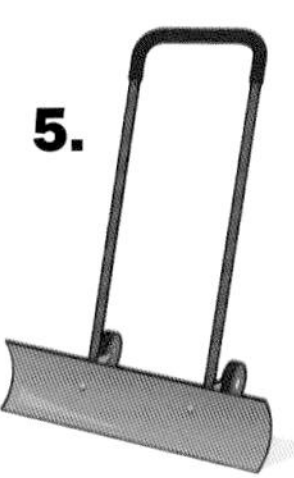

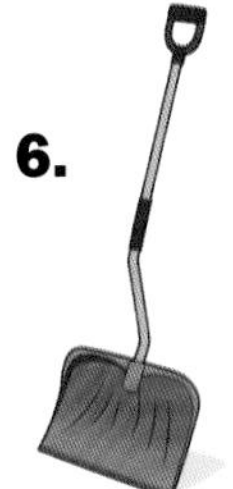

© Kate Francis, Brown Bird Design

While some states stall out in a snowfall, Minnesota's 1,700 snowplows and 200,000 to 300,000 tons of salt get us back in business while other states are spinning their wheels. The Minneapolis/St. Paul airport rarely closes.

© Jim Gehrz, 2013, Star Tribune

MN
#1

The Hottest Place on Earth

On July 19, 2011, Moorhead was the hottest place on Earth. **Hotter than any place in Africa or India.**

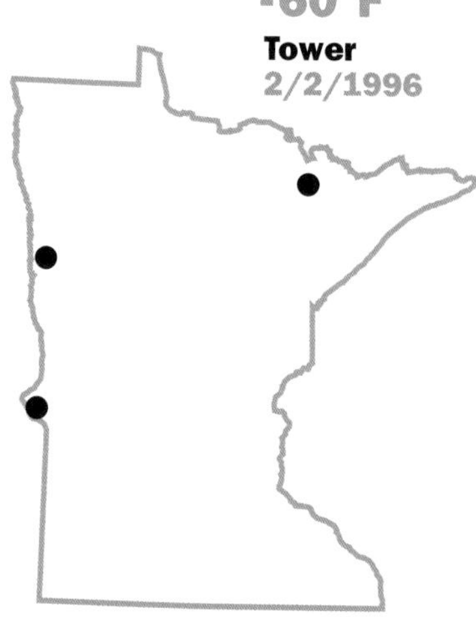

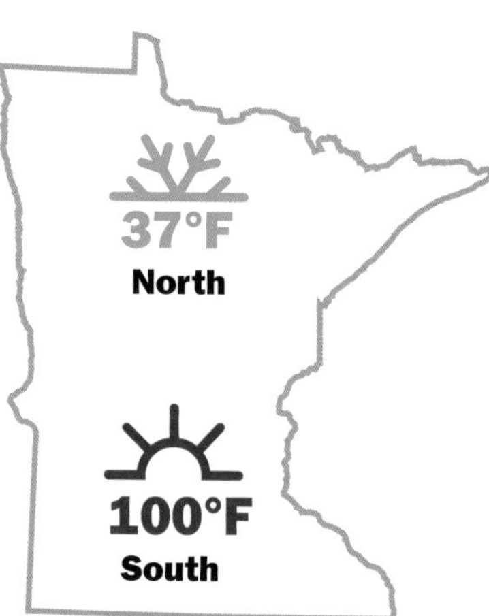

MN
#3

Coldest States:

1. Alaska
2. North Dakota
3. **Minnesota**
4. Maine
5. Wisconsin

Coldest and Hottest Days

Minnesota is known to be a cold state. Most non-residents think it is colder than it actually is. Weather reporting stations over 300 miles north of the Twin Cities report temperatures that could be 30° colder than those in other cities.

MN
FACT

The greatest recorded difference in temperature on the same day was 100° in the south to 37° in the northeast, a difference of 63°.

top 10 MN

Given the number of cold days (Denver has more freezing days than the Twin Cities), you'd think the state would empty out. But **Minnesota is in the top 10 of the "stickiest."** 66% of the people who are born here or move here...stay here.

Source: Dr. Myles Shaver, Carlson School of Management

Freeze to Death...
Not Likely

Of all weather-related deaths from tornadoes, hurricanes, lightning, flooding, and extreme cold, heat is the quietest and most prolific killer. In 2015, 130 U.S. deaths were due to extreme heat.

Source: New York Times *6/21/2015*

A Bad PR Day

On January 9, 2016, the NFL playoff game was held at the TCF Bank outdoor stadium, where the temperature at game time was -2°. The world saw the Twin Cities at their coldest when, on average, there are only eight days a year when the temperature at midday drops below zero degrees.

MINNESOTA
VIKINGS

© Dan Anderson

© Max Haynes/mxfotos.com

How much time do we actually spend outside? Unless you have an outside job (construction, for example) you spend the vast majority of your life inside. If you sleep eight hours, work eight hours, and spend time dining, driving, or watching TV, you only have a couple of hours a day left for other activities like going to a concert or game . . . or making a snow angel.

MN FACT

In Minnesota, 55,000 children (both boys and girls) play hockey.

© Shutterstock

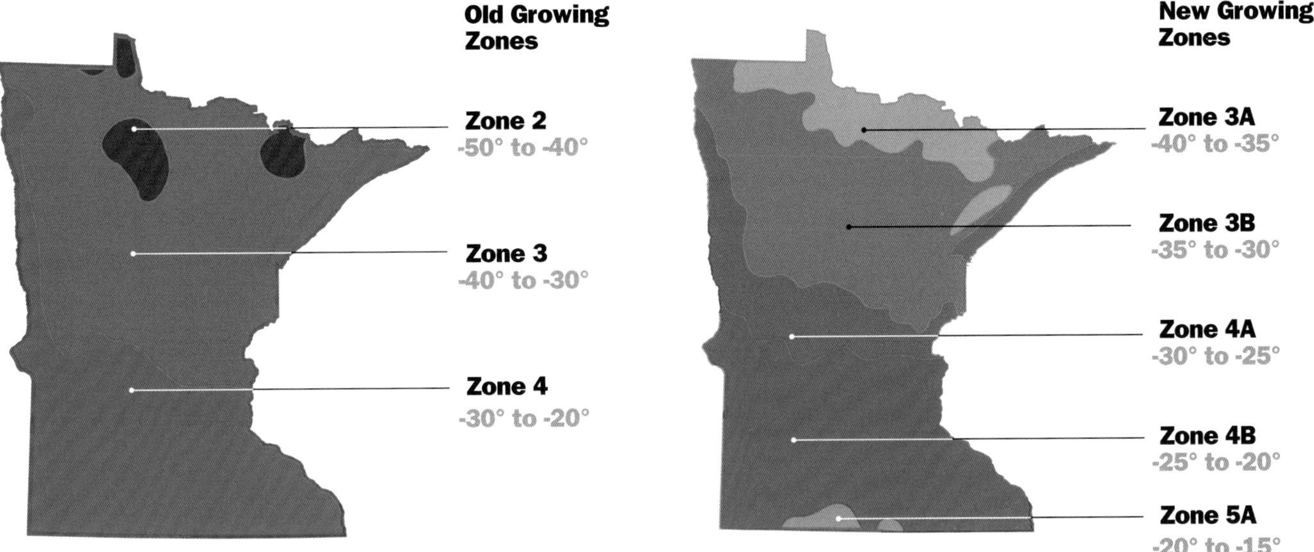

The Future of Winter

Numbers tell the story. Winters really are getting warmer. Scientists attribute the upward climb in winter low temperatures to global climate change. This upward trend has been most apparent in the last 35 years.

On the bright side, a change in growing zones for planting vegetables and flowers gives many an earlier start in spring.

Metro Warming

Parking lots, roads, and rooftops have created a "heat island" in the Twin Cities where temperatures are 5 to 10° warmer than other parts of the state. Surprisingly, hot days in July and August won't be getting hotter due to high moisture levels, which limit how hot or cold it can get.

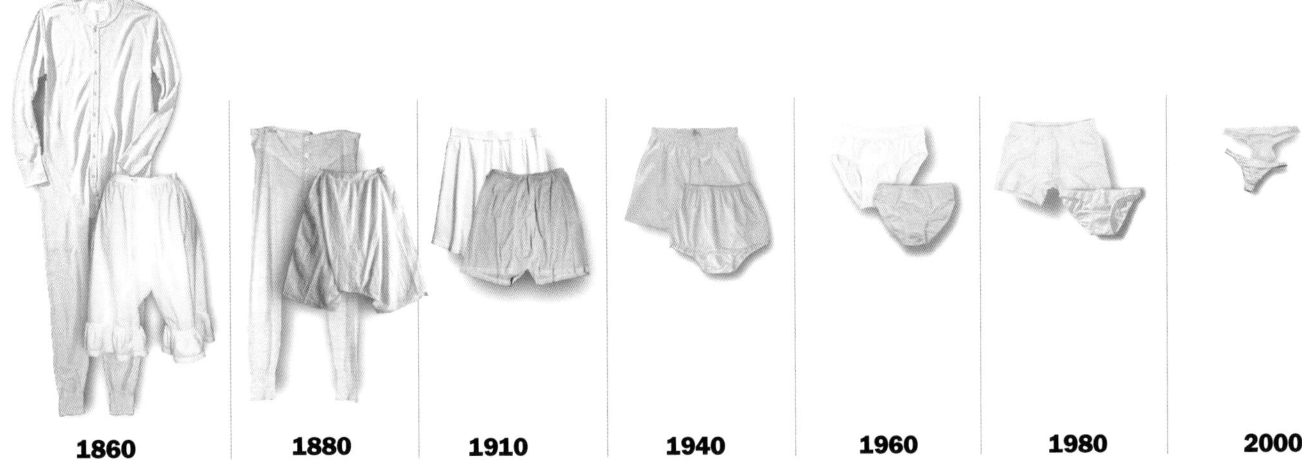

Revealing New Evidence of Global Warming

Renee Jones Schneider, ©2015, Star Tribune

World's Largest Skyway System

In 1958, architect Ed Baker came up with a novel idea: an elevated tunnel to connect two of his buildings so his tenants could go between them without going outside. Today, a network of 11 miles of multitiered skyways covers downtown Minneapolis. Downtown St. Paul has five miles. Some 150,000 downtown workers and thousands of guests stay warm in the winter and cool in the summer traversing these skyways. The explosion of high-rise housing in the inner city can also be attributed somewhat to the presence of the skyway system.

Mall of America

On very cold days or very hot days, many families enjoy the temperature-controlled interior of the Mall of America. The nation's largest mall, it has more than 500 stores. An indoor amusement park and adjacent water park are popular with both children and adults. Early in the morning, you will find "mall walkers" getting exercise by walking miles of hallways.

©Jordan Stead/seattlepi.com

MN FACT

The Mall has the fifth-largest K-9 corps in the nation, with 15 dogs. New York City is #1.

© Katie Weisbecker

Embracing Winter

You can flee from winter, hide from it, or embrace it. Minnesotans engage in more than 20 different winter sports and activities, ranging from popular cross-country skiing to snowmobiling. Four of the more unusual winter activities begin with ice.

© Caters News

Ice Fishing

Thousands of fishermen and women compete for cash prizes for the biggest catch in dozens of contests throughout the state. Some are snug in a homelike fish house while others rough it by sitting out in the open.

Wikimedia commons

Ice Boating

With little snow on the lake and a stiff wind, ice boaters come out in droves to drive their boats at speeds from 68 mph up to 100 mph for larger boats. Hang on!

© Dan Anderson

Red Bull Crashed Ice

In a competition called ice skating on steroids, skaters test their skill and daring on a steep downhill twisting track, dotted with jumps and rollers, in front of the Cathedral of St. Paul. Thousands come to watch the chaos.

© REUTERS/Alamy

Pond Hockey

Each winter more than 2,000 athletes and teams come to Lake Nokomis in Minneapolis to compete in the U.S. Pond Hockey Championships.

© Greg Lundgren/www.GregLundgrenPhotography.com

MN
#1

St. Paul Winter Carnival

It's the nation's oldest and largest winter festival. Events include parades, cultural celebrations, ice and snow sculptures, and a giant snow slide. Rice Park in downtown St. Paul becomes a magical place when the ice sculptures are lit.

City of Lakes Loppet ▶

The Loppet is a great urban cross-country ski festival right in the heart of Minneapolis. A 26k race is one of many events, including fat tire racing, speed skating, skijoring (dogs pulling skiers), and the Luminary Loppet: an enchanted evening of bonfires, ice sculpture, hot cider and neighborhood get-togethers all happening on Lake of the Isles.

©2015 Steve Kotvis, f/go (www.f-go.us)

©2015 Steve Kotvis, f/go (www.f-go.us)

©2014 Steve Kotvis, f/go (www.f-go.us)

© Ray Klempka

Winter Eyes, by Linda Barrows

Winter lays hand to Minnesota sooner than anyone wishes. Lush green leaves dry in the warm September days as we jog and walk and watch for red and orange hues. "We won't have many more days like this" is a lament with the surety of experience behind it: we know our skies. "Getting away anyplace warm this winter?" people begin to ask each other, and themselves. Many flee to lands still colored by summer. Yet those of us who root here during winter are rewarded with a sense of beauty refined. Emerging from December's monochrome landscape, the eye discerns a gentler source of awe. Gray morning light has a soft sheen through the clouds, lustrous and perfect as a pearl. Tree bark, hardly ever noticed, captures attention with taupe mottled grooves and brown mosaics. Nightfall comes later by mid-January, and a pale pink breaks over the sky, backed by tender mauve deepening to slate. February evenings, a coral tinge ebbs toward the horizon as the sun's final rays wash through the window panes, announcing daylight's end. Arctic afternoons cut gold shafts of light through crystalline blue skies, setting millions of snowflakes to sparkling like jewels along the ground's white unbroken surface; icicles twinkle among green pine boughs, suspended as if from a massive chandelier, and our own resilience fills each heart. Minnesota's winter tones hold beauty lost to those who escape the cold, best seen—and understood—through winter eyes.

As temperatures rise around the world, water and its heightened scarcity will become increasingly more sensitive politically and economically. Minnesota's abundance of water is likely to become an even more treasured resource.

Lake Okabena hosts a national windsurfing competition.
Source: Star Tribune *6/12/14*

Chapter 3.
Water, water, water in a world short of water.

"Minnesota's water future looks positive due to our continuous investment in clean water and a traditional respect for water conservation."

Dr. Deborah Swackhamer

Professor of science, technology and public policy, Hubert Humphrey School of Public Affairs, and former chair of the Science Advisory Board of the U.S. Environmental Protection Agency

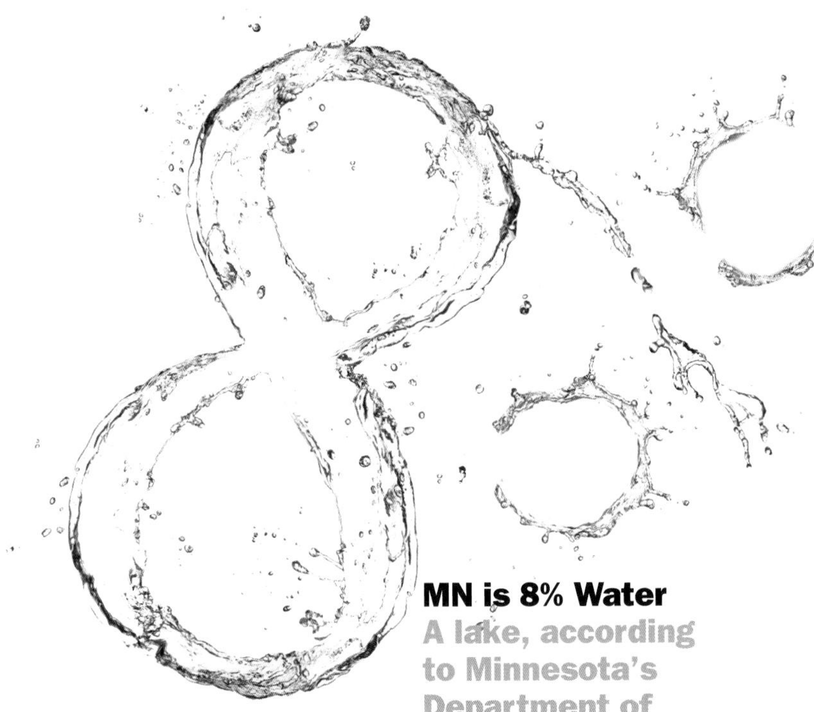

MN is 8% Water

A lake, according to Minnesota's Department of Natural Resources, is a body of water 10 acres or more in size. Minnesota is not the land of 10,000 lakes. There are 11,842 lakes in Minnesota, plus 69,200 miles of rivers and streams, of which 589 miles are designated as wild and scenic rivers.

© Brian Peterson, Star Tribune

In April 2016, Minnesota's Governor Mark Dayton made water quality and availability his #1 priority. The Minnesota Legislature recently passed legislation creating more and larger protection zones from agricultural runoff around creeks, rivers, and even some ditches.

© Fotosearch

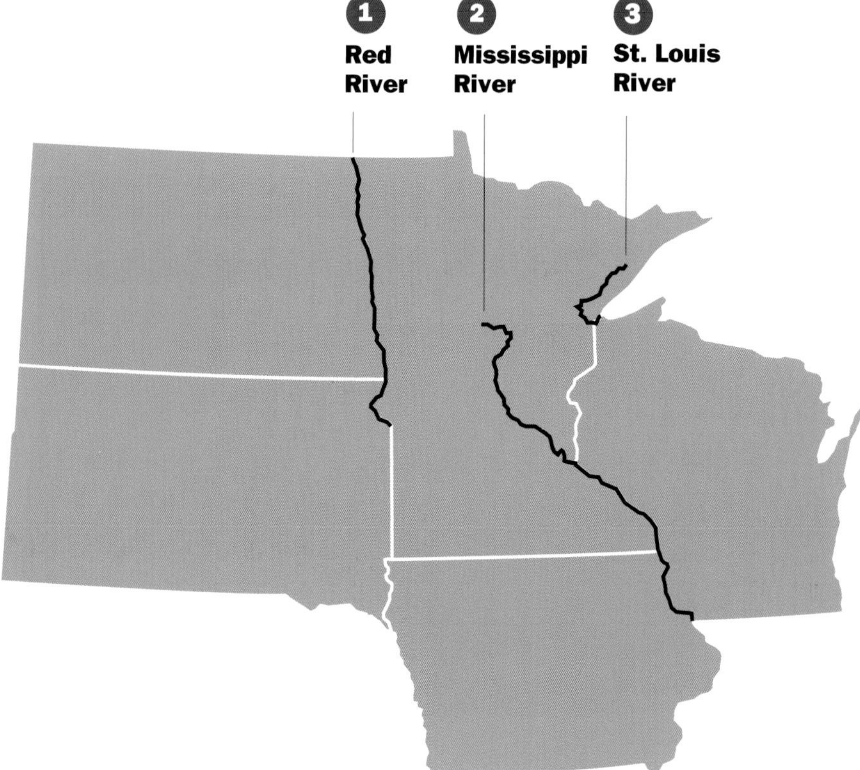

Three Headwaters

Minnesota is the only state with three major headwaters: the Red River flowing into Canada, the Mississippi River flowing into the Gulf of Mexico, and waters supplying Lake Superior. Minnesota is also the only state with a plan to maintain and fix water infrastructure with a dedicated fund to preserve, protect, and enhance its water over time.

Lake Itasca

Courtesy of MN DNR

The origin of the "Father of Waters," the mighty Mississippi River, is Lake Itasca in Itasca State Park in north central Minnesota. There you can easily walk across the source of the great Mississippi, but at its widest navigable point the river is two miles across. It's the nation's second-longest river, providing recreation, transportation and drinking water on its 2,340 miles to the Gulf of Mexico.

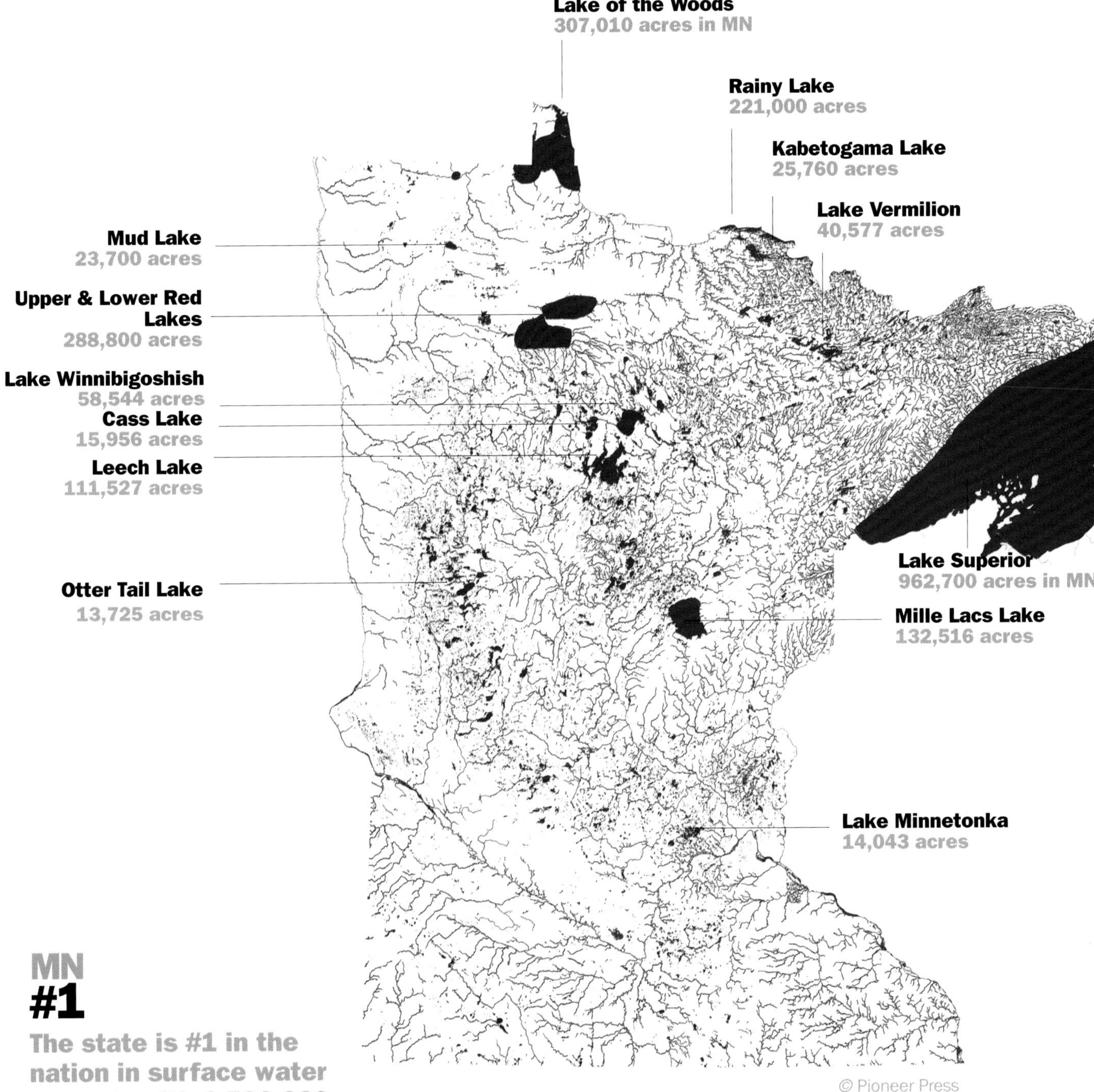

© Pioneer Press

MN
#1

The state is #1 in the nation in surface water acreage with 2,500,000 acres, if wetlands are included in the total. The state's aquifers, although reduced somewhat, are in the best condition in the nation.

© Dan Anderson

MN #3

Almost one million acres of Lake Superior, the world's third-largest body of freshwater by volume, are bordered by Minnesota on its famous North Shore. Only Lake Baikal in Siberia and Lake Tanganyika in Tanzania are larger. Surprisingly, Lake Superior is so large it has inland tides. And it holds 10% of the world's fresh water.

MN FACT

Lake Superior holds three *quadrillion* gallons of water! If that much water was spread across both North and South America it would cover the land in a foot of water.

Source: MN Sea Grant

Superior Water Could Be Sold to Dry States... if It Wasn't Illegal

The Great Lakes Compact prohibits the transfer of water to any unit of government, individual, or corporation. Its creation put an end to someone's pipe dream to build a pipeline to sell Superior water to Arizona.

© Cherezoff/Shutterstock

MN
FACT

Minnesota has more miles of shoreline than Hawaii, California, and Florida combined.

Source: chrisfinke.com 12/30/16

St. Louis Park Water

In a small Twin Cities suburb there is something in the water. Norm Ornstein, Al Franken, the Coen brothers, Thomas Friedman, Susan Segal, and Steve Goldstein all lived within blocks of each other.

3/8 of 1%

The Legacy Amendment

In 2008 Minnesota voters took a bold and historic action by imposing a three-eighths of one percent tax on themselves each year for 25 years, until 2034, in the name of cleaner water, healthier habitat, better parks and trails, and sustaining the state's arts and cultural heritage. Five years later that tax had generated a dedicated fund of more than a billion dollars.

Minnesota has taken action to establish sustainable water quality goals and standards. Through a citizen-supported amendment to the state's constitution, the unique Clean Water and Land Legacy Fund became the envy of other states.

Minnesota has not been immune to the degradation of surface water that every place in the world faces. Southern Minnesota has hundreds of lakes (by Minnesota standards) endangered by algae growth caused by multiple sources, the biggest being agricultural (pesticide and fertilizer) runoff from corn and soybean crops grown in the state. Growing corn and soybeans is not only water intensive but also consumes large amounts of energy and fertilizer.

© istock

© Vasyl Torous/Alamy

© Ron Nykamp

© Karen Melvin

Lake Minnetonka

Located just 20 minutes from the central business district of Minneapolis, the Minnetonka shoreline has some of the largest homes (often called McMansions) in the region. The most expensive sold in 2015 for $23 million. Lake Minnetonka gets heavy recreational use. Its 14,000 acres and hundreds of miles of shoreline have 10,000 private boat docks. 60,000 boats use the public marinas every summer. Sailing regattas, power boats, water skiers, canoes, kayaks, and paddleboards can be seen every day on the lake from April till late October. Lake Minnetonka is also one of the premier fishing lakes in Minnesota.

MN FACT
Waterskiing was invented on Lake Pepin in 1922.

© Dan Anderson

Although Texas claims to have more lakes than Minnesota, Doyle Cole of Lubbock summed up the Texan definition of a lake when he said, ***"Heck, anything that stays wet more than nine months a year down here is a lake."***

© Associated Press

MN FACT

The air in the BWCA is so pure planes are not allowed to fly below 4,000 feet over it.

© Tom Bean

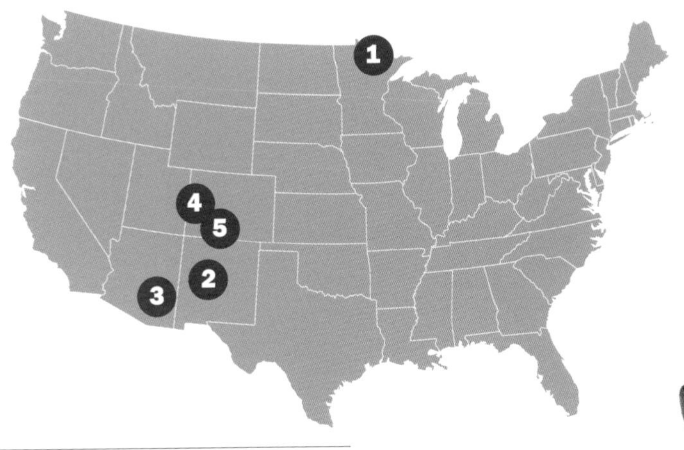

MN
#1

Top U.S. Wilderness Areas:

1. Boundary Waters Canoe Area, MN
2. Sandia Mountain, NM
3. Pusch Ridge, AZ
4. Maroon Bells–Snowmass, CO
5. Sangre de Cristo, CO

On the Canadian border, the Boundary Waters Canoe Area hosts 250,000 visitors annually. It is comprised of 1,000 pristine lakes with more than 1,200 miles of overland canoe routes, 11 hiking trails, and approximately 2,000 campsites.

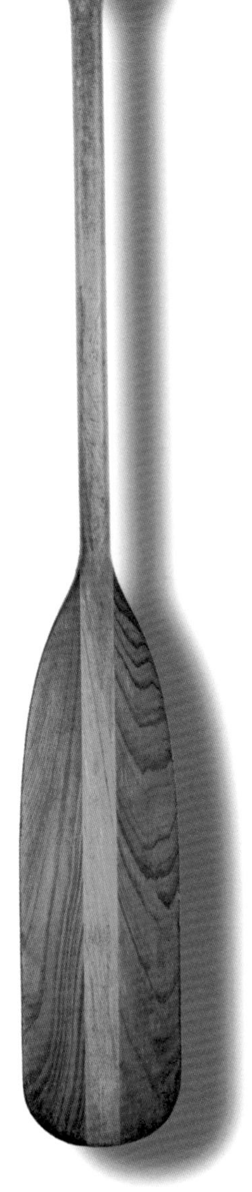

The BWCA also has some of the oldest rock formations on Earth, estimated to be at least 2.7 billion years old. Nearby Voyageurs National Park attracts an additional 240,000 visitors annually.

Are there any big fish left, or have they all been caught? Not long ago two monster fish were caught on Mille Lacs Lake just 17 days apart.

On Thanksgiving eve 2015, a lunker muskie estimated at 61 pounds was caught by Dominic Hoyos of Stillwater, possibly eclipsing the world record fly-fishing muskie caught by Robert Hawkins just 16 days earlier, also on Mille Lacs.

Source: Star Tribune

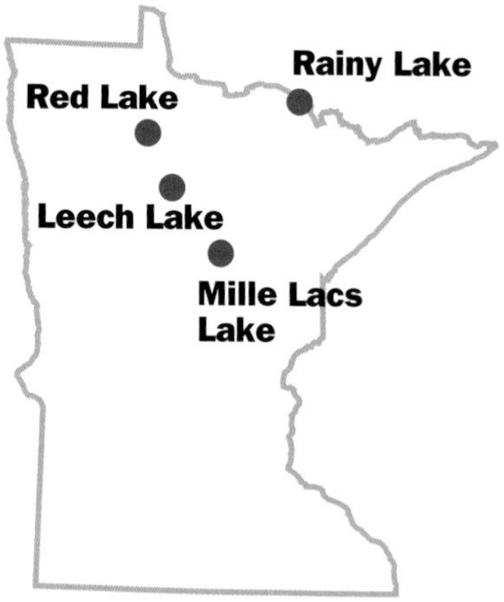

Red Lake
Rainy Lake
Leech Lake
Mille Lacs Lake

Mille Lacs Lake in central Minnesota, and Red Lake, Leech Lake, and Rainy Lake in the north, are a few of the most prolific producers of game fish.

Lonny Hess of White Bear Lake caught a 46-inch muskie off this very dock on Lake Harriet in 2015.

© Jon Luke

© Michael Masser-michaelmasser.co.uk

© Greg Bentz

Until recently, both Minneapolis and St. Paul had turned their backs on the mighty river that flows right through each downtown. Now each city has massive redevelopment plans for their riverfronts that will make them recreational treasures.

© Steven Gaertner

The St. Croix, a wild and scenic river, might be the National Scenic Riverway closest to a major city in the U.S. It is a canoe-lover's favorite. Less than an hour from the Twin Cities you can find yourself on flowing water flanked by tall Norway pines and populated by a multitude of eagles and ospreys.

No large boats, waterskiing, or Jet Skis are allowed on the upper St. Croix. The St. Croix is composed of 181 miles of protected scenic waterway and 19 miles reserved for outdoor recreation.

© Greater MSP

MN
#7
Wind Energy

Minnesota was an early adapter of wind energy technology. It currently ranks seventh in wind energy production, with Texas in the #1 position. However, the state ranks fourth for having 15% of its electricity generated by wind.

MN
#3
Most Energy Efficient:

1. New York
2. Vermont
3. **Minnesota**
4. Wisconsin
5. Utah

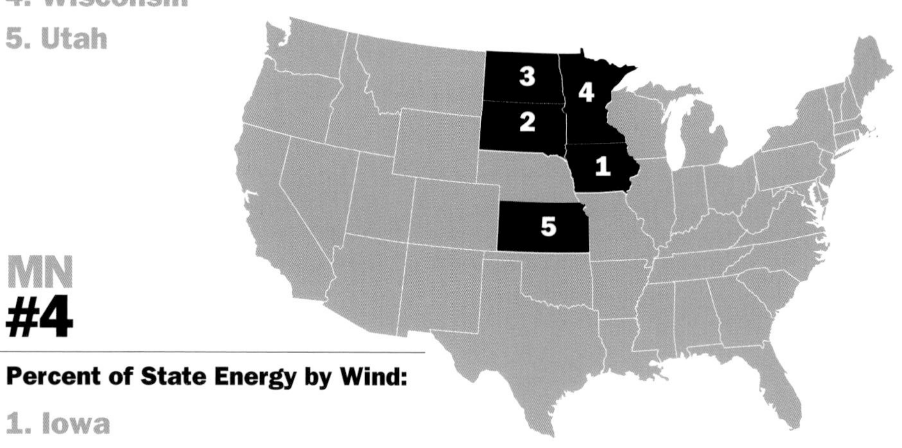

MN
#4
Percent of State Energy by Wind:

1. Iowa
2. South Dakota
3. North Dakota
4. **Minnesota**
5. Kansas

The Good Air

EPA studies show the Twin Cities with six days of unhealthy air for sensitive groups vs. 57 days in Phoenix, 30 days in Houston, and 96 days in Los Angeles. Minnesota is not in the top 25 states for the worst air.

© Shutterstock

MN
#1

Overall Environmental Quality:

1. Minnesota
2. Vermont
3. Washington

Source: WalletHub 2016

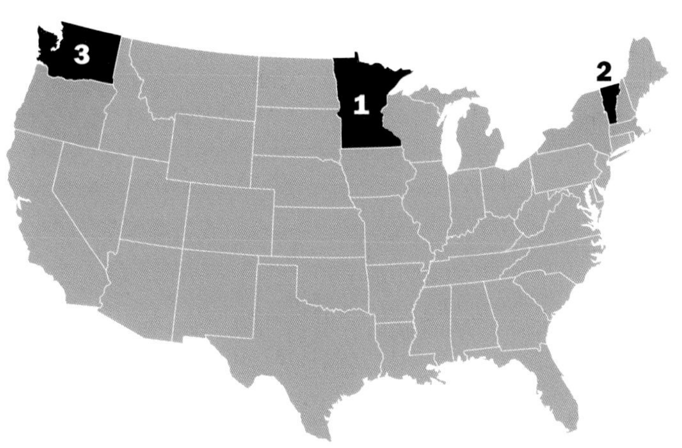

© Shutterstock

Target is #1 in the nation for using the most solar power, while Ecolab (#50) and General Mills (#69) made the list of the 100 most sustainable companies in the world. Only three other U.S. companies ranked higher than Ecolab.

MN
#1

Minneapolis ranks first in the nation in percentage of commercial space with a green designation.

Source: multihousingnews.com/cities

Minnesota ranks 10th in LEED-certified buildings, according to the U.S. Green Building Council. The Butler Building in Minneapolis was the first century-old building to be LEED certified.

Mortenson Construction's renewable energy group is the nation's largest wind energy contractor and the third-largest solar contractor.

Source: Engineering and News Record *2017*

MN
#4

Environmental Sensitivity:

1. Iowa
2. South Dakota
3. North Dakota
4. Minnesota
5. Kansas

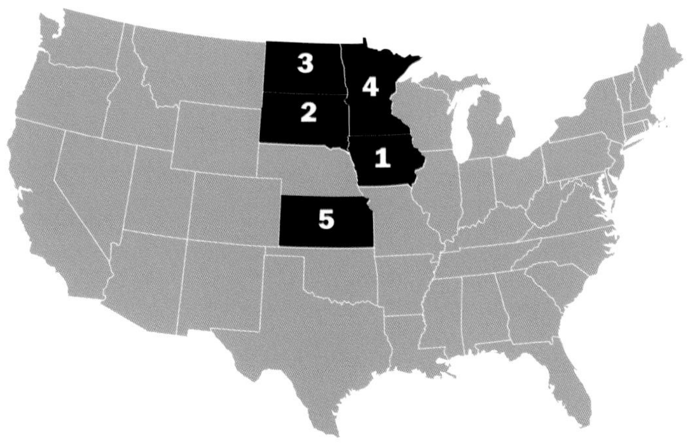

MN
#2

Percent of Recycled Municipal Waste:

1. Maine
2. **Minnesota**
3. Arkansas & California
4. New Hampshire

Minnesota is Positioned to Become the National Leader against Climate Change

Even before the onset of mandatory requirements, Minnesota put in place one of the most, if not the most, rigorous renewable energy standards in the country, requiring that 25% of the state's power come from sources such as wind, solar, and hydrogen by 2025. The state has also reduced emissions from power plants by 20% in the past 10 years. Minnesota Senator Al Franken believes that Minnesota's lack of fossil fuels and abundance of brainpower means it's uniquely positioned to take advantage of what he and others see as the new energy economy.

Source: MinnPost *Dec. 2015*

25%
alternative

20%
reduction

©Lights & Shadows Pte Ltd/Amoeba Digital Imaging

Twin Cities 16th in Traffic Congestion

"The Twin Cities will be better off in the future than other congested cities. Many can't expand due to mountains or water. Others may not have the political will or financial strength to mitigate the problem. It will take both new high-occupancy lanes and transit to ward off these problems."

Charles Zelle
Minnesota's Commissioner of Transportation

The new $1.6 billion Los Angeles freeway expansion showed that simply adding more highways is not the answer. It was congested on opening day.

© Photobank gallery/Shutterstock

MN
#1

The American Public Transportation Association named the Twin Cities 2016 Transit System of the Year.

© Nerthuz/ShutterStock

MN
#2

The Twin Cities rank #2 in large cities for the percentage of the population that either works from home or walks, bikes, carpools or travels by public transit to work. Some 5% commute by bicycle. Cincinnati is #1.

Source: NerdWallet/greenest cities

MN
#3

There is no shortage of water, boats, or fish.

States with the largest boat registration:

1. Florida
2. California
3. Minnesota
4. Wisconsin
5. New York

© Edmont

Chapter 4.
Get up off the couch.

© Jeff Wheeler, 2007, Star Tribune

MN
#1

World's Largest Amateur Sports Facility

The National Sports Center in Blaine (a Minneapolis suburb) has more than 50 grass soccer fields, an 18-hole golf course, an 8-sheet ice arena, a cycling velodrome, and 100,000 square feet of indoor training and meeting space. It hosts the Schwan's USA Cup, the largest youth soccer tournament in the western hemisphere.

© Carlos Gonzalez, 2014, Star Tribune

© Carlos Gonzalez, 2014, Star Tribune

National Sports Center

52 Outdoor Soccer Fields
Also used for other sports, such as rugby, lacrosse and ultimate disc

Sports Expo Center
18,000 square feet (approximately 33 yards by 60 yards) of turf activity area

NSC Velodrome
50 meters of all-wood cycling track, pitched 42° in the corners

NSC Stadium
8,500 seats

Sports Hall
FieldTurf® surface with 58,350 square feet (approximately 60 yards by 100 yards) of activity area

Schwan Super Rink
Eight sheets of ice, largest ice arena complex in the world

Victory Links Golf Course
Minnesota's only PGA Tour–designed course open to the public

Courtesy of National Sports Center

© Greg Ryan/Alamy

MN FACT

Theodore Wirth Park, a mile from downtown Minneapolis, is a bit smaller (by 84 acres) than the 843-acre Central Park in New York City.

© Scott A Schneider Photography

MN FACT

95%

of Minneapolis residents live within a 10-minute walk of a park.

MN #1&2

Best City Park Systems:

1. **Minneapolis**
2. **St. Paul**
3. **Washington, DC**
4. **Portland**
5. **San Francisco**

Minneapolis was recently named as having the best park system for the third year in a row.

Best Botanical Garden

The Minnesota Landscape Arboretum was voted best botanical garden in an April 2017 *USA Today* survey. The New York Botanical Garden finished #2.

Minnehaha Falls Regional Park, South Minneapolis
© Greg Lundgren Photography >

Not only did the original planners designate ample space for parks of all types, they also preserved the inner-city lakes by preventing the sale of lakeshore to private parties. Most city lakes have three lanes around them for biking and walking.

MN
#1&2

Not only are the Twin Cities the best for biking, they are also the second best for bike safety.

Source: bicycling.com/new/top/50

Biker's Bonanza
Minneapolis has more than 120 miles of on- and off-street bicycle facilities, making it the most bike-friendly city according to *Bicycling Magazine*. Not only are the Twin Cities the top biking cities in the U.S., they also rank **#22 in the world among bike-friendly cities** like Amsterdam and Brussels. The only other city in North America to make the list was Montreal, Canada.

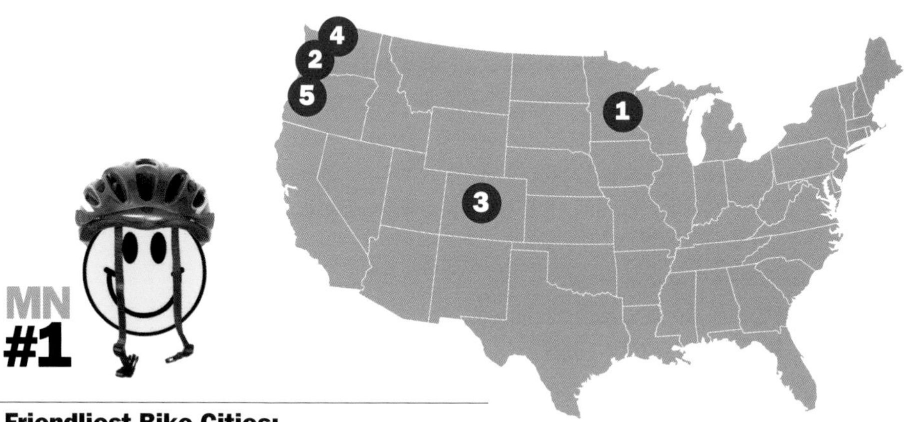

MN
#1

Friendliest Bike Cities:

1. **Minneapolis**
2. Portland
3. Boulder
4. Seattle
5. Eugene

MN
x5

How Dense Can We Be?
With five times the national median for lane and path density, Minneapolis has the densest biking network in the nation, 32% ahead of Boston, its nearest rival. And Minneapolis is only halfway to its goal of 402 miles of bikeways.

Source: Star Tribune *3/10/16*

200 Nice Ride locations for short-term bike rentals are heavily used by both local residents and tourists.

A hot new sport for a cold day, fat tire biking is the fastest growing winter sport in the state.

© Hansi Johnson

The entire state has capitalized on the popularity of biking by creating 590 miles of paved trails.

© Paul Pluskwik, IRRRB

Minnesota Wins Best Trails State Award

It has 1,266 off-road trail miles, 785 miles of natural surface trails, 22,000 miles of snowmobile trails, 1,000 miles of equestrian trails in state parks, 1,000 miles of off-highway vehicle roads, plus 1,300 miles of off-highway vehicle trails in state parks.

Source: americantrails.org

Arctic Cat, Inc.
Plymouth, MN

Courtesy of Arctic Cat

MN FACT

It's not surprising, given the popularity of snowmobiling, that Polaris Industries and Arctic Cat are headquartered in Minnesota and sold over $15 billion in off-road vehicles between 2013 and 2015.

Polaris Industries
Medina, MN

© Polaris Industries Inc.

MN #10

Minnesota ranks 10th in the nation for motorcycle registrations.

Indian Motorcycle Manufacturing Company
Medina, MN

© Polaris Industries Inc.

6%

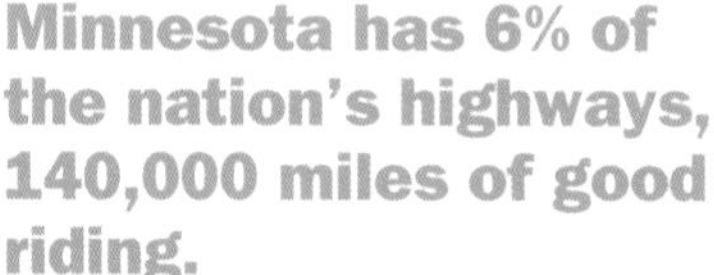

Minnesota has 6% of the nation's highways, 140,000 miles of good riding.

Tonka Toys
formerly of Mound, MN

© Ray Ross

© Polaris Industries Inc.

It's hard for many to imagine that you can be comfortable, even sweating, while driving a snowmobile at 40 mph at 10° above zero. Newly developed snowmobile gear, including heated handlebars, has great body heat retention capabilities, adding comfort to the popularity of the sport.

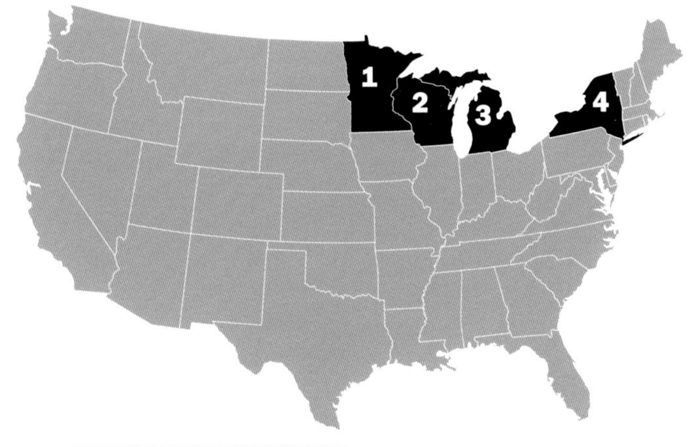

MN
#1

Snowmobile Ownership:

1. Minnesota – 258,000
2. Wisconsin – 237,000
3. Michigan – 205,351
4. New York – 115,982

© paul@competitiveimage.us

1|4 MN

The Vasaloppet is a grueling 598-km cross-country ski race that draws racers from all over the world to Mora, MN. It is one of four locations worldwide for the famous traditional Swedish race. The others are Sweden, Japan, and China.

1 2 3 4

Mora

MN #1

World's largest summer artificial ski run.

Courtesy of Buck Hill

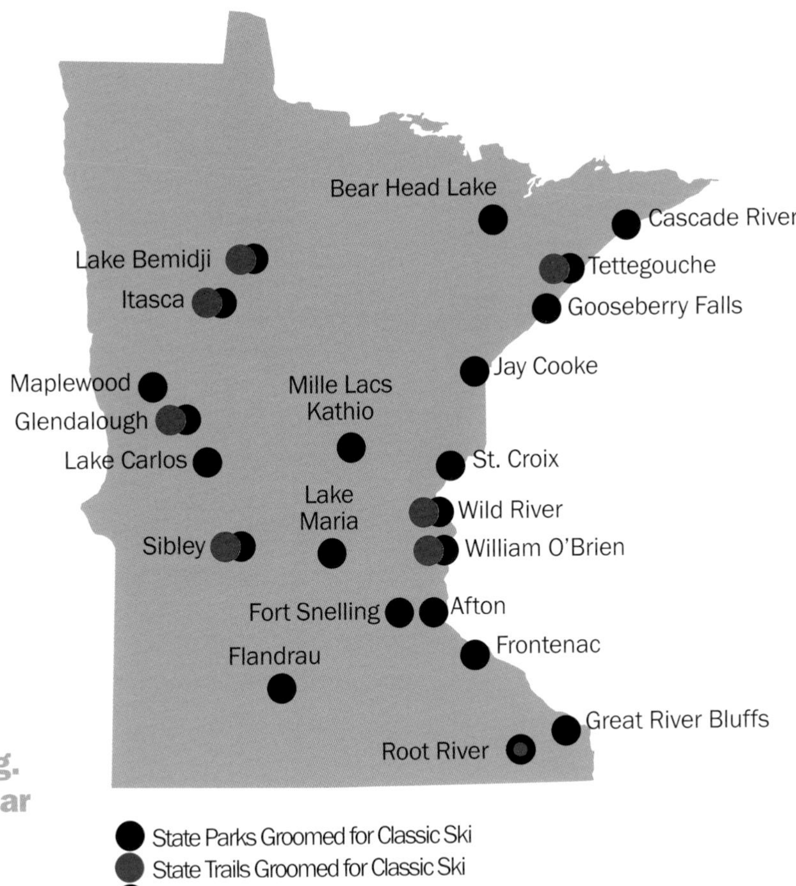

Minnesota maintains 350 miles of cross-country ski trails. The trails are machine groomed and used for touring and ski skating. Night skiing is a popular pastime.

Public Domain

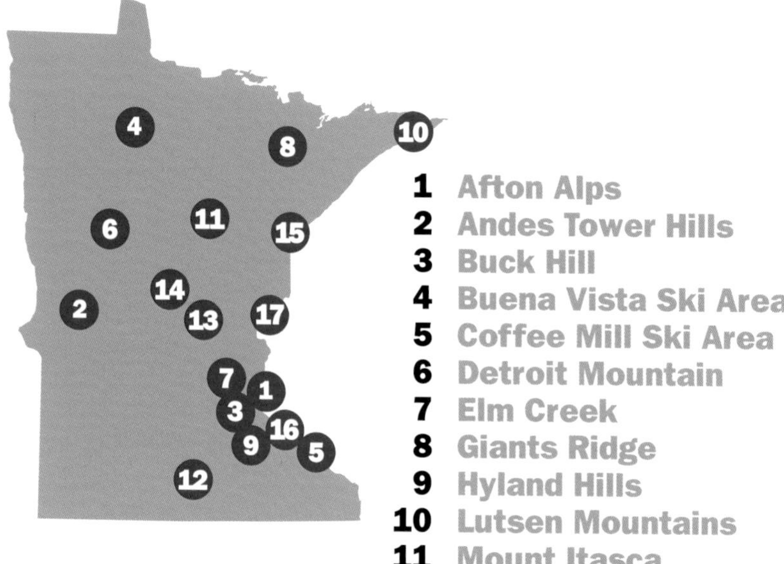

1 Afton Alps
2 Andes Tower Hills
3 Buck Hill
4 Buena Vista Ski Area
5 Coffee Mill Ski Area
6 Detroit Mountain
7 Elm Creek
8 Giants Ridge
9 Hyland Hills
10 Lutsen Mountains
11 Mount Itasca
12 Mount Kato
13 Mount Ski Gull
14 Powder Ridge
15 Spirit Mountain
16 Welch Village
17 Wild Mountain

Lutsen Mountains, located on the shore of Lake Superior, has the longest ski run between Vermont and Colorado, with an elevation of 875 feet and several runs longer than a mile.

© Lutsen Mountains

In 2016 more than 30,000 runners competed in the Twin Cities Marathon, which is sponsored by Medtronic. The marathon begins in Minneapolis and ends in St. Paul, skirting parks, lakes, and rivers, and is commonly called the most beautiful urban marathon in America.

© Dan Anderson

Fifteen of the 162 species of fish found in Minnesota waters

Muskellunge

Northern Pike

Walleye Pike

Lake Trout

Largemouth Bass

Brook Trout

Rainbow Trout

Brown Trout

Smallmouth Bass

White Crappie

Black Crappie

Perch

Green Sunfish

Bluegill

Pumpkinseed

MN #3

A million and a half fishing licenses are issued annually in Minnesota, third only to Texas and California. The licensed fishermen and women are after 162 species of fish found in 5,500 Minnesota lakes producing almost 10 million pounds of fish annually.

Source: Minnesota Department of Natural Resources

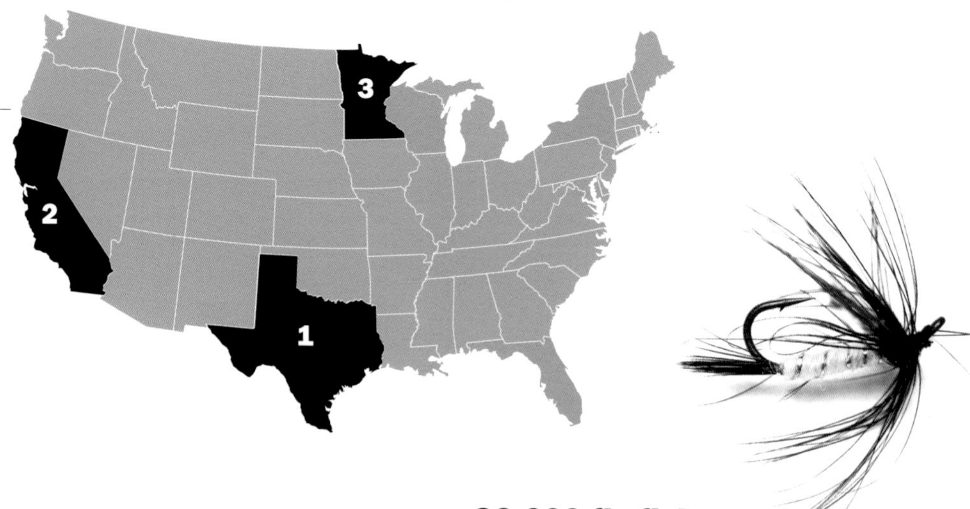

90,000 fly fishermen will be found on the shores of 69,000 miles of rivers and streams in the state.

© TOSP/Shutterstock

© 2016 Corey Gaffer Photography

Ice fishing seems to tourists and newcomers (as well as a few locals) a peculiar pastime. Some icehouses have kitchens, satellite dishes, and wall-to-wall carpeting (with a few holes cut into it). In Minnesota you can even get a mortgage on an icehouse.

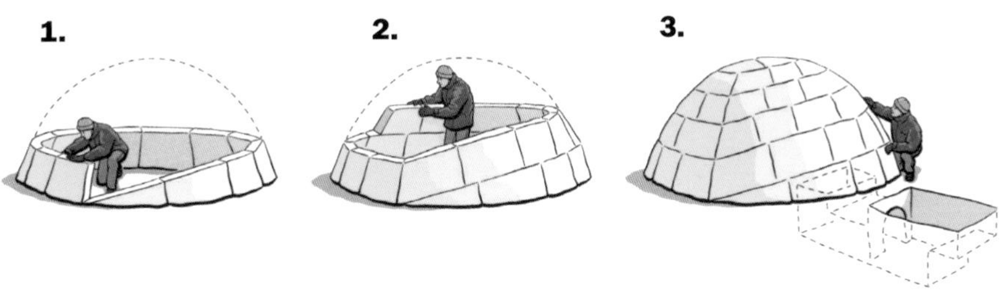

How to build an icehouse . . . ohhh shoot, wrong kind of icehouse.

© Robert L. Prince

Thousands of ice fishermen and women compete for big dollars in 66 ice fishing contests annually with purses worth thousands of dollars. Some sit for hours in the open, staring down a hole.

© John Overland

Special voyageur canoe and paddleboard tours have helped bolster attendance.

Itasca State Park, located in northern Minnesota, has more than 37,000 acres and 100 lakes. Here the Mississippi River begins its grand journey of 2,552 miles to the Gulf of Mexico. While other states are experiencing a downturn, Minnesota State Park visits were up 20% in 2014. Eight million people visited the system, which consists of more than 600 miles of paved roads and trails and 74 parks.

© Underworld/Shutterstock

Minnesota State Parks

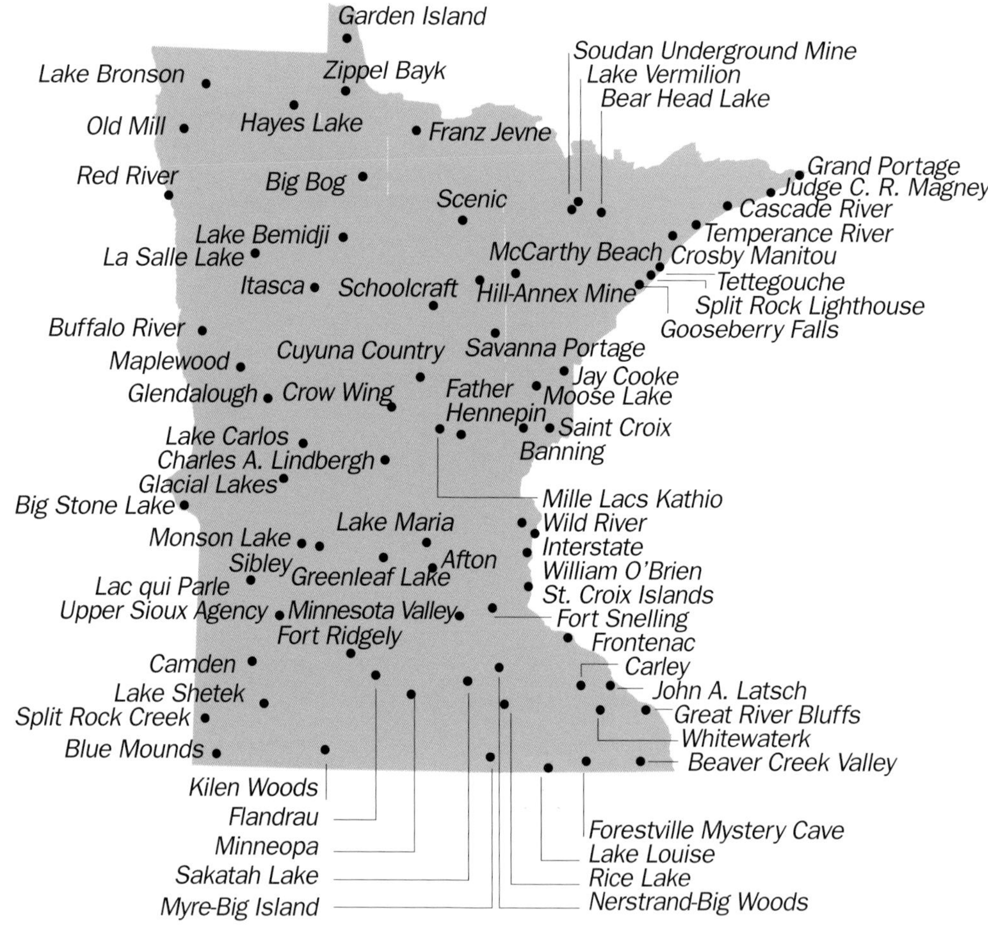

MN #2

At the headwaters of the Mississippi River is Itasca State Park, the second-oldest park in the U.S.

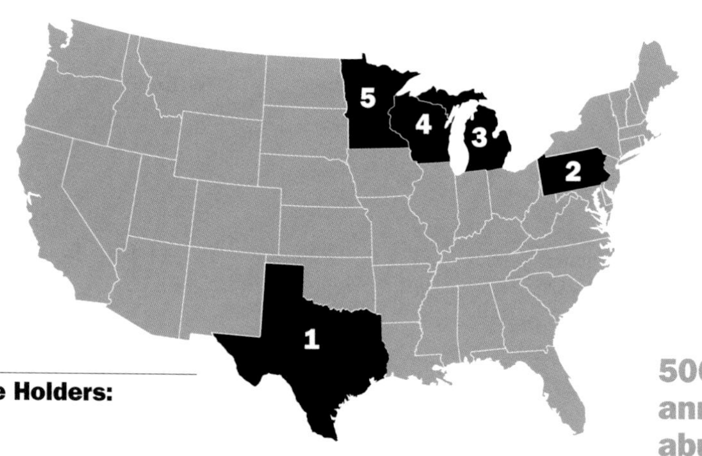

MN
#5

Top Hunting License Holders:

1. Texas
2. Pennsylvania
3. Michigan
4. Wisconsin
5. **Minnesota**

500,000 hunters annually pursue the abundant white-tailed deer in the woods and fields of Minnesota. Ruffed grouse is the most popular upland game bird sought by hunters. 80,000 hunt for ducks, 75,000 hunt for pheasant, and 40,000 hunt for wild turkey.

© *Dave Orrick*, Pioneer Press

There is Always a Cabin in the Woods

Minnesotans love leaving town for a weekend and going to a cabin "up north." It's often hard to find an employee at work on Fridays in the summer. They have either rented a cabin on a lake or own one of the 120,000 in Minnesota and 40,000 in western Wisconsin. Many are winterized for year-round use.

© Paul Crosby

MN FACT %

5.1

A 2011 study by the U.S. Census Bureau's Housing and Household Economic Statistics Division found that 5.1% of Minnesota homes are cabins.

© John Linn/Adventure Studios

WHERE LEGENDS ARE FORGED
SAMSUNG
OMEGA
Standard Life Investments

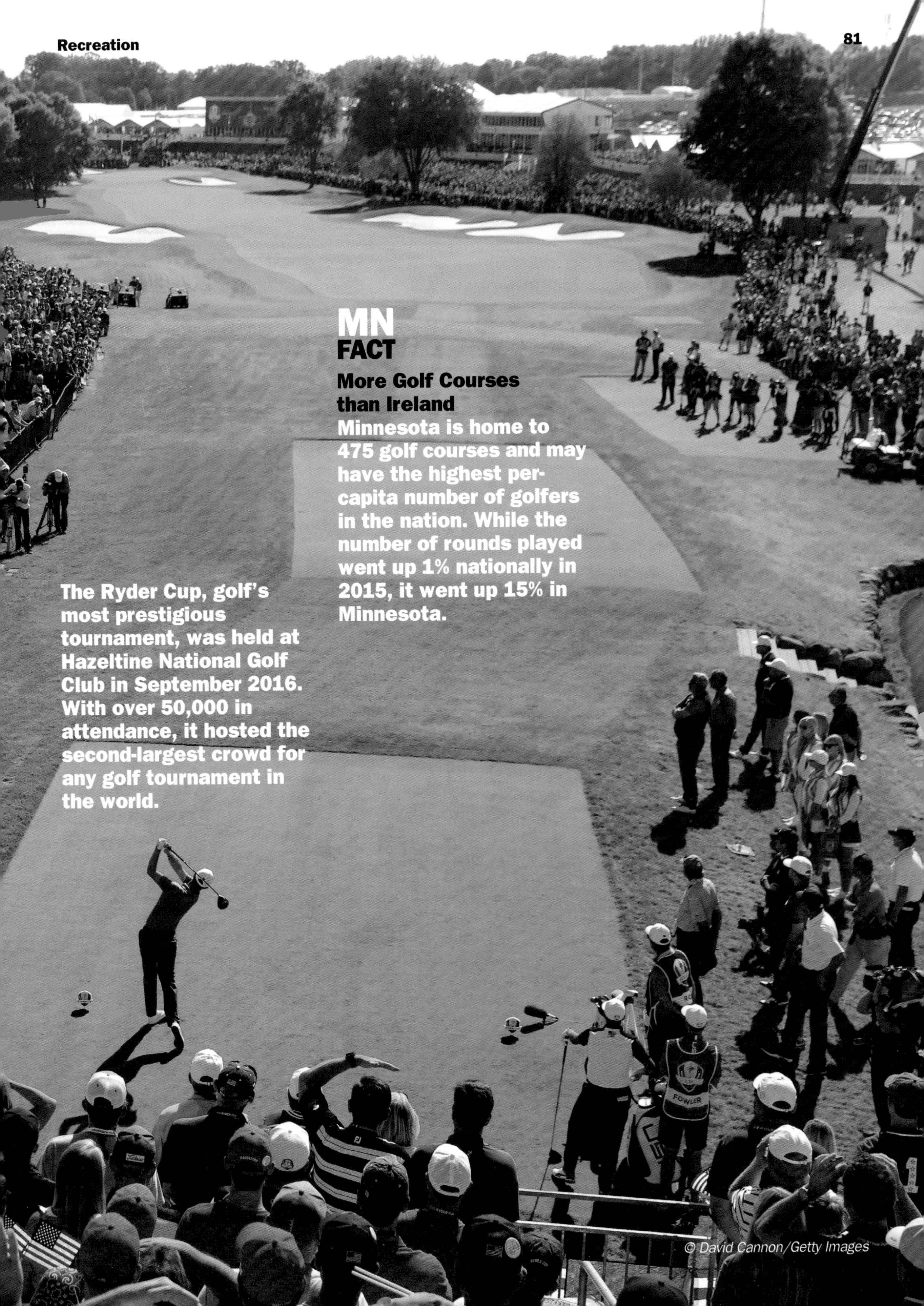

MN FACT

More Golf Courses than Ireland

Minnesota is home to 475 golf courses and may have the highest per-capita number of golfers in the nation. While the number of rounds played went up 1% nationally in 2015, it went up 15% in Minnesota.

The Ryder Cup, golf's most prestigious tournament, was held at Hazeltine National Golf Club in September 2016. With over 50,000 in attendance, it hosted the second-largest crowd for any golf tournament in the world.

Long Live Minnesotans

Yes, it's true. Minnesota is #1 in the nation for male life expectancy and #2 for women.

Source: worldlifeexpectancy.com/usa/life)

© Squaredpixels

Chapter 5.
Big hearts. Long livers.

How Minnesotans Roll.

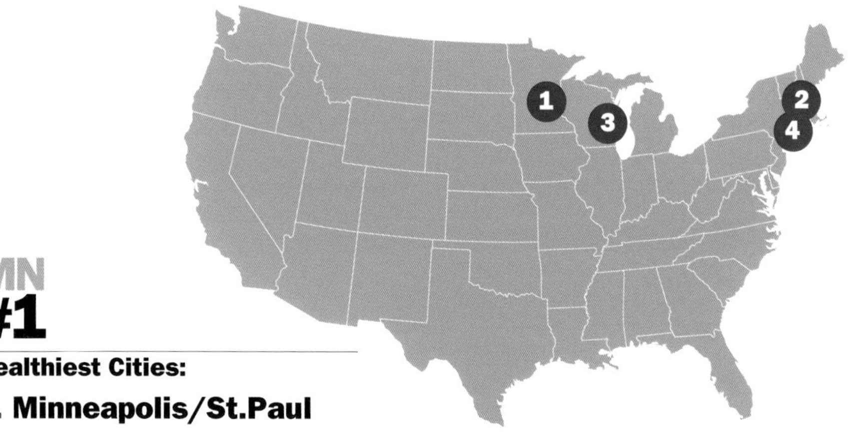

The combination of a healthy environment, healthy lifestyles, and world-renowned health care has always put Minnesota at the top of the list for wellness.

MN
#1

Healthiest Cities:

1. **Minneapolis/St.Paul**
2. Cambridge
3. Madison
4. Bridgeport

Source: Livability.com

3
MN

The infant mortality rate is low in Minnesota (the state ranks 11th in the nation). It is one of the top three states for children's vaccination rates. The Twin Cities have three excellent children's hospitals plus two hospitals specializing in children with physical disabilities.

Source: Statstica 2017

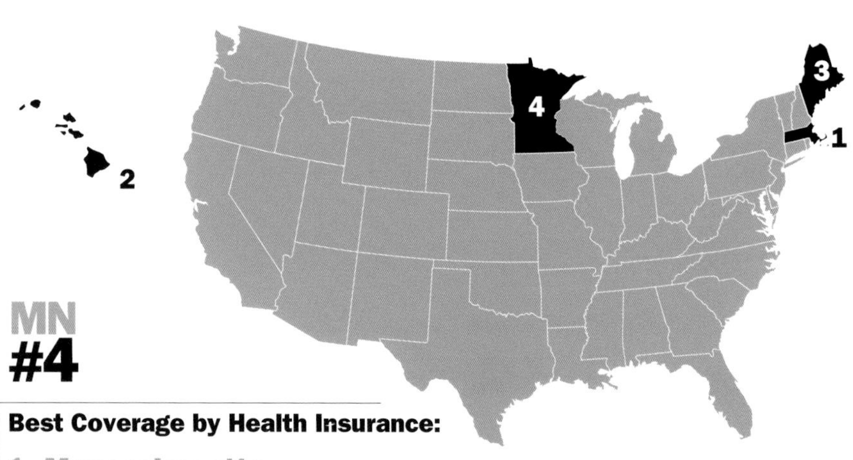

MN
#4

Best Coverage by Health Insurance:

1. Massachusetts
2. Hawaii
3. Maine
4. **Minnesota**

© Dreamstime

80% of the state's population gets at least 30 minutes of exercise daily.

Source: Livability.com

It is not uncommon for your friends to drop by and invite you to exercise with them. Minnesota ranks #2 in the American fitness index and third overall in health.

Source: americanfitnessindex.org
Source: United Health Foundation

patience

patients

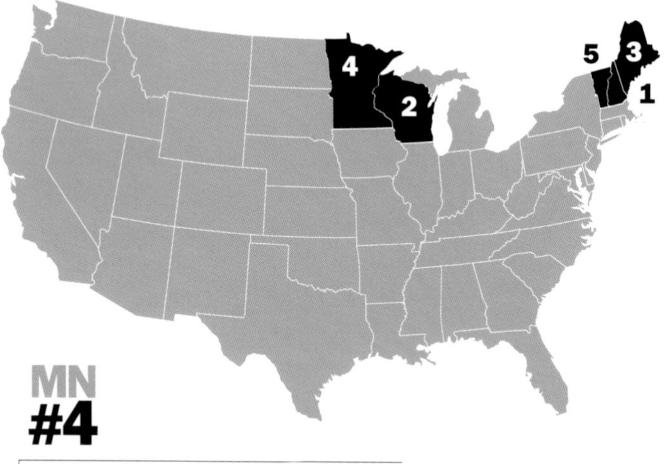

MN
#4

Shortest State Waiting Times:

1. New Hampshire
2. Wisconsin
3. Maine
4. **Minnesota**
5. Vermont

Source: vitals.com

If you do get sick, you won't have to wait too long to see a doctor.

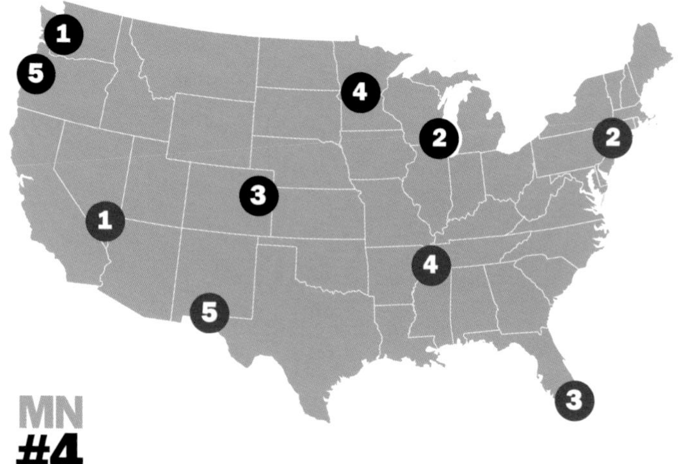

MN
#4

Shortest City Waiting Times:

1. Seattle
2. Milwaukee
3. Denver
4. **Minneapolis**
5. Portland

Source: vitals.com

Longest City Waits:

1. Las Vegas
2. New York City
3. Miami
4. Memphis
5. El Paso

MN
#1

MAYO CLINIC

If you have an unusual sickness you can go to the Mayo Clinic, ranked #1 in the nation. Others in the top tier: (not in order) Mass General, Cleveland Clinic, Johns Hopkins, and UCLA Medical Center.

Source: U.S. News & World Report, *2014–2015*

The Mayo Clinic is located about 90 minutes south of the Twin Cities. In 2015, 1.3 million patients from all 50 states and 140 foreign countries were treated by 4,500 staff physicians and scientists. Overall, the clinic employs 64,000 people. In addition, the Mayo Medical School, a graduate school, and a school of health sciences are also located in the complex.

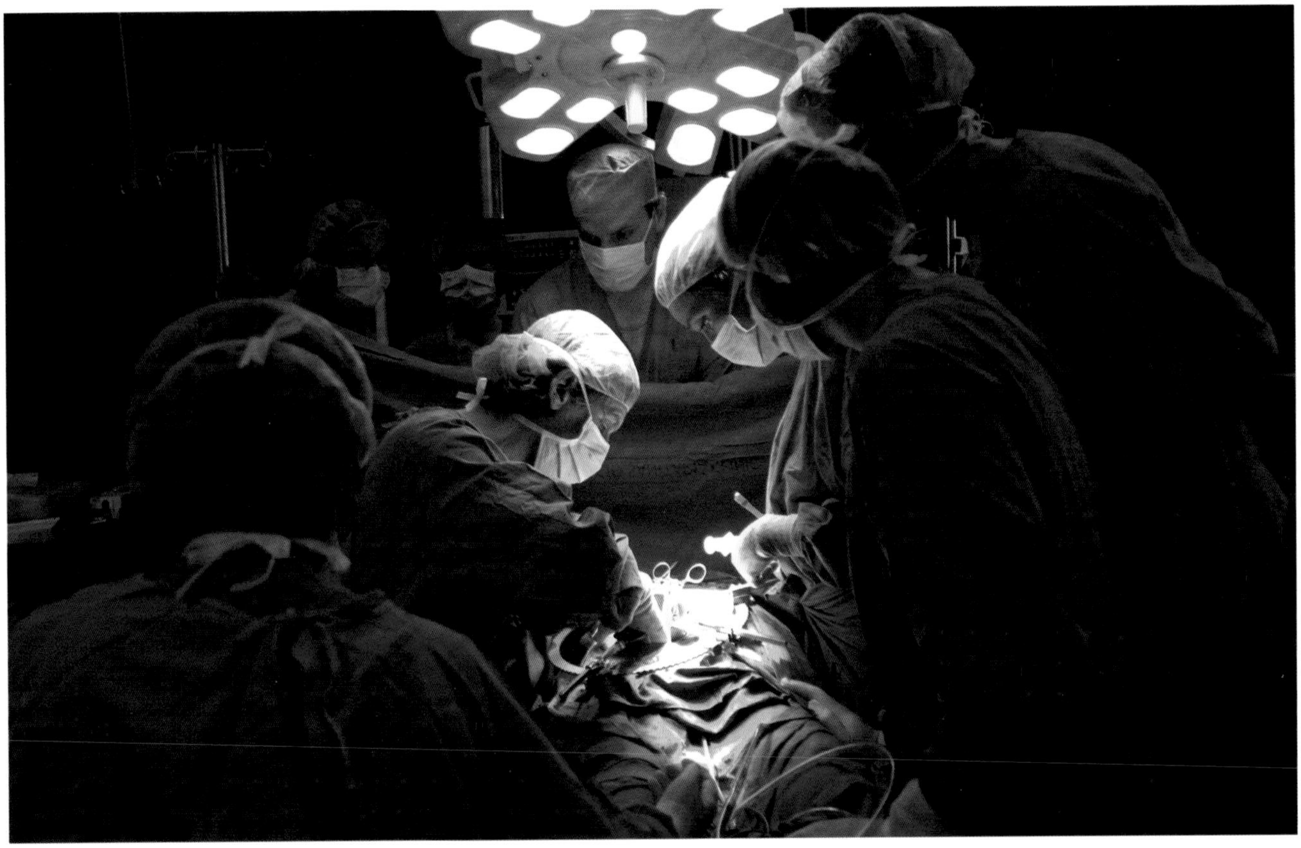

© Tino Soriano, National Geographic

Artist's Rendering © Perkins Eastman

MN FACT The $6.5 billion planned expansion of the Mayo Clinic in Rochester will make it the dominant health center in the world.

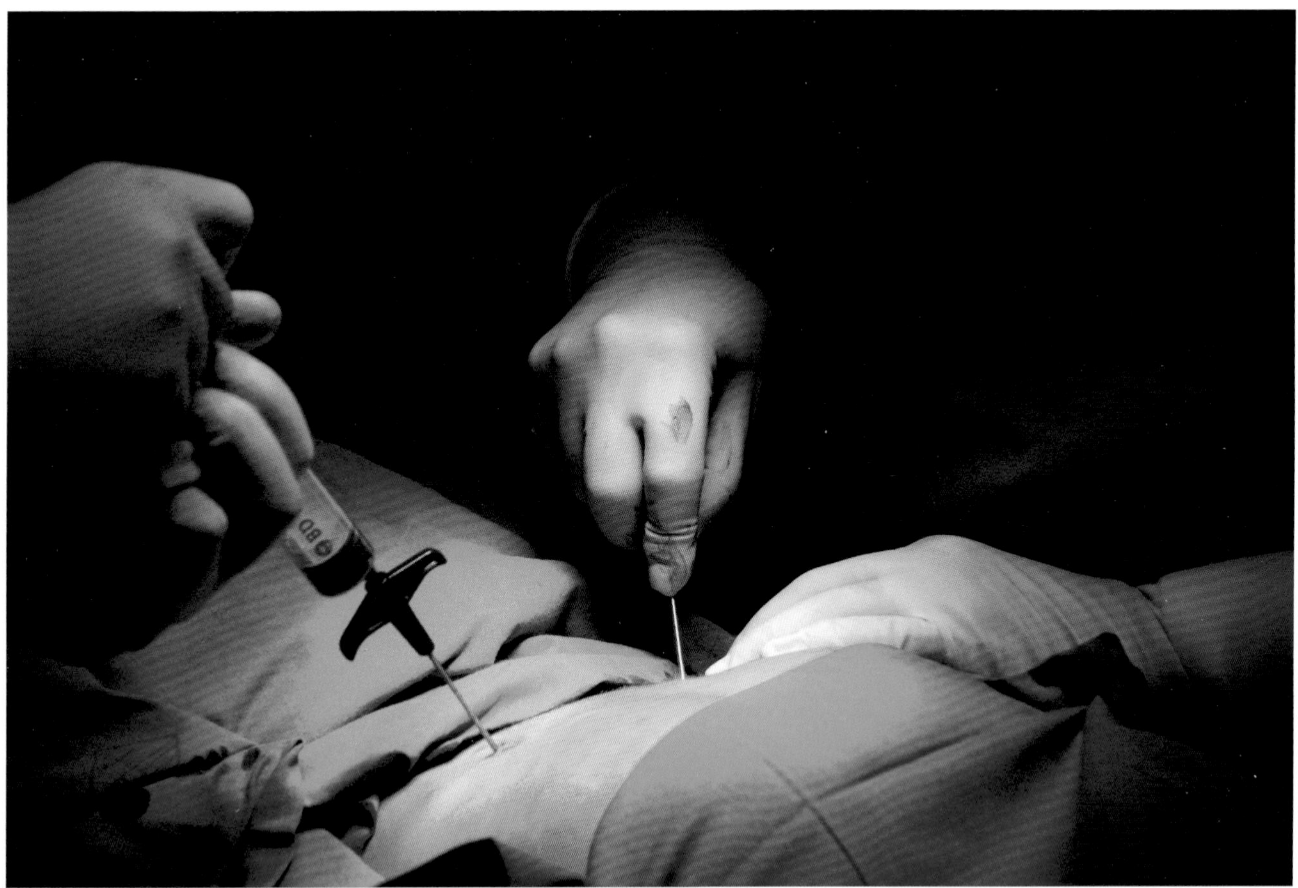

© *Tino Soriano,* National Geographic

MN
#1&10

The University of Minnesota is a major medical research institution. The first open-heart surgery and first bone marrow transplant were performed there, and it is in the top 10 in the world for HIV/AIDS research.

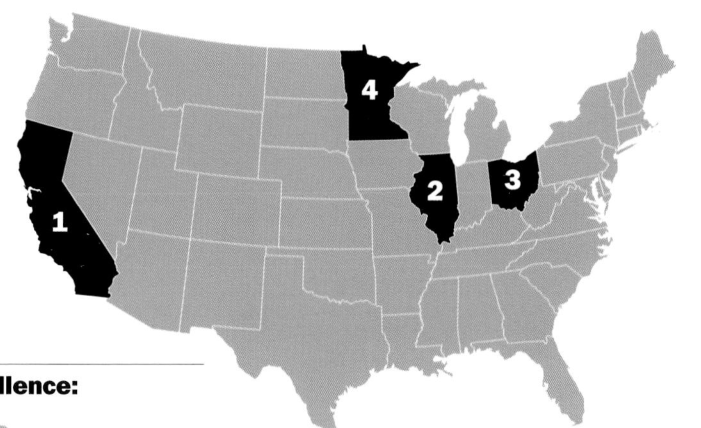

MN
#4

Hospital Excellence:

1. California
2. Illinois
3. Ohio
4. **Minnesota** (#1 per capita)

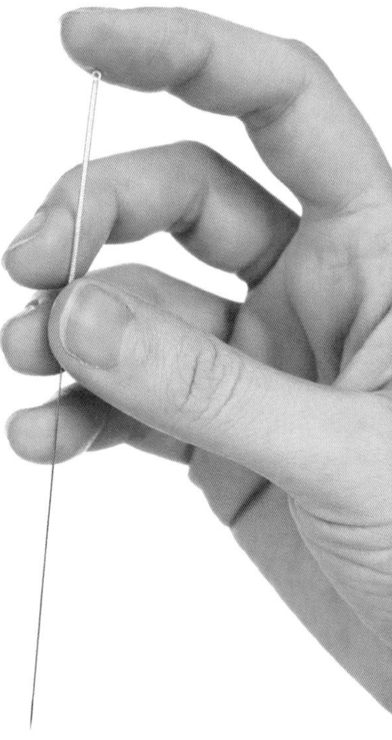

ABBOTT NORTHWESTERN HOSPITAL

MN
#1&4

Abbott Northwestern Hospital and the Heart Hospital in Minneapolis see 48,000 patients annually. Abbott, along with six other hospitals in the nation, received Truven Analytics' top ranking. **Minnesota ranks #1 per capita and fourth overall in hospital excellence, with seven hospitals in the top 100.**

The Virginia Piper Cancer Institute at Abbott Northwestern has the highest cancer survival rate in the country. The American College of Surgeons Commission on Cancer ranked VPCI **#1 of 74 programs nationwide** and granted it an outstanding achievement award.

Penny George Institute for Health and Healing is the largest systemwide integrative medicine program in the nation.

Courtesy of Piper Breast Center

The Most Quiet Place on Earth

If you need peace and quiet, come to Minnesota, which houses the quietest place on Earth. Built by Orfield Labs, the Anechoic Chamber is a room within a room within a room using 3.3-inch-thick fiberglass acoustic wedges, double walls of insulated steel, and foot-thick concrete walls to stop sound. It is used for acoustic testing. People begin to hallucinate after 45 minutes of total quiet in the room.

brake

break

If you are worried about being in a car crash, you should know that Minnesota is the safest state in the nation.

Source: carinsurancecomparison.com

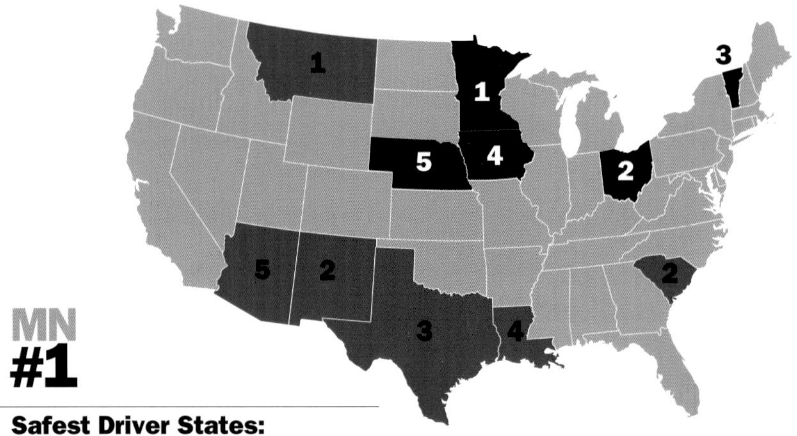

MN #1

Safest Driver States:

1. **Minnesota**
2. **Ohio**
3. **Vermont**
4. **Iowa**
5. **Nebraska**

Worst Driver States:

1. **Montana**
2. **South Carolina/New Mexico**
3. **Texas**
4. **Louisiana**
5. **Arizona**

Source: carinsurancecomparison.com

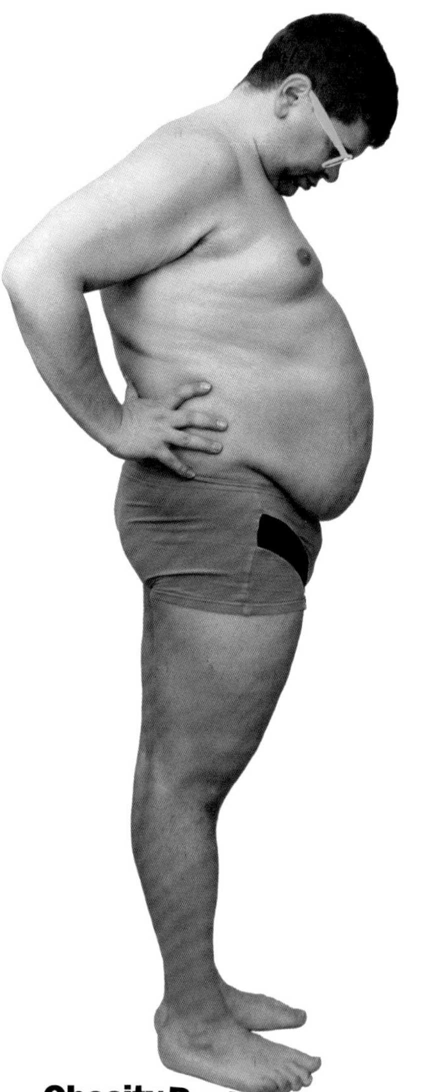

MN
#4

Reducing Obesity:

1. New York
2. Montana
3. Ohio
4. **Minnesota**

Minnesota is one of four states to reduce its obesity rate. New York, Montana, and Ohio were also among the first to go down rather than up in rate of obesity. In spite of the recent success, Minnesota is only the 11th-skinnest state.

Source: Trust for Americas Health

Obesity Ranking:
Minnesota ranks #39 on an obesity scale, with approximately one in four residents classfied as obese. Mississippi ranks #1 with one in every three people deemed obese. Colorado has one of every five.

Source: Robert Wood Johnson Foundation

MN
#1

If you are tired, you have another reason to come to Minneapolis. It ranks #1 in sleep with about 23 days per month of good sleep. Overall happiness and low unemployment are among the reasons for a good night's sleep.

Source: bestplaces.netdocs/studies/ ambiensleep.aspx

MN
#6

Planned Parenthood of Minnesota, North Dakota and South Dakota is the sixth-largest affiliate in the nation, providing many low-income women with health services.

Public Domain

Minnesota is not in Tornado Alley, but it does experience an average of 45 touchdowns annually. (There were 1,700 touchdowns in the U.S. in 2011 and 935 in 2013.) Texas, Florida, and Oklahoma are usually especially hard hit. Minnesota is also not in a lightning corridor.

Less Smoke Gets in Your Eyes

Minnesota is in the top 10 states with low smoking rates. Minnesota led the country in the fight against tobacco. Winning the lawsuit *State of Minnesota, et al. v. Philip Morris, et al.* was called one of the greatest health achievements of the 20th century.

© 123RF

Land of 10,000 Treatment Centers

The world-renowned Hazelden Betty Ford Foundation for addiction treatment and advocacy has spawned numerous other centers.

The Enormous Impact of the Health Care Industry in Minnesota

The combination of the largest health insurance company in the nation (UnitedHealthcare), the highest concentration of medical technology companies in the nation (400), **the nation's #1–rated hospital (Mayo Clinic)** sitting in a vast medical complex in Rochester, and a large medical, teaching and research university has created thousands of high-paying jobs with more to come in the future.

MN
#4

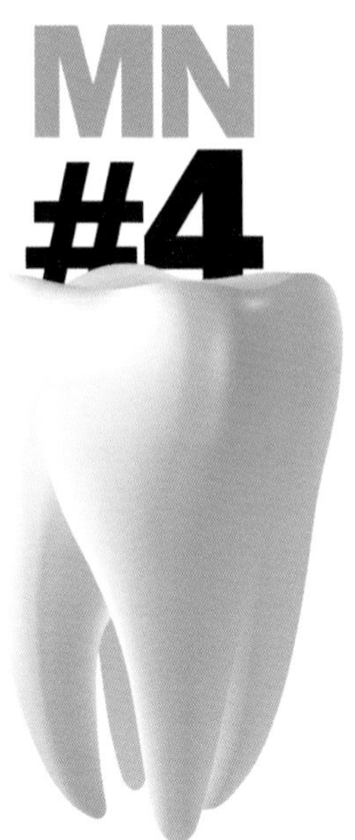

Toothache?
Not to worry. Minnesota is in the top 10 for dental care.

Source: huffingtonpost.com

MN
#1

Top Seismically Quiet Places:

1. **Minnesota**
2. Amazon Basin
3. Western Sahara
4. Southwestern Africa
5. Parts of Antarctica

Quake Phobia?
Central Minnesota is the safest place from earthquakes in the world. No mudslides, hurricanes, cyclones, tidal waves, tsunamis, sandstorms, or ocean flooding in Minnesota.

Faith in the Police:

In a survey of attitudes toward police conducted by Harper Polling of Pennsylvania, 90% of the respondents from Minnesota indicated they approved of or strongly approved of the way their "local" police force handles its job. 85% of Minnesotans feel safe walking their streets at night.

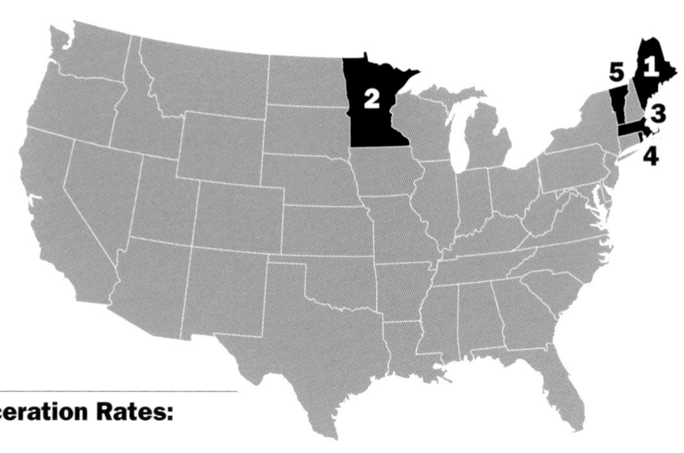

MN
#2

Lowest Incarceration Rates:

1. Maine
2. **Minnesota**
3. Massachusetts
4. Rhode Island
5. Vermont

Low Incarceration Rate

Even with the recent rise in the number of adults being locked up, Minnesota is #2 in low incarceration rates.

Source: Wikipedia 2015

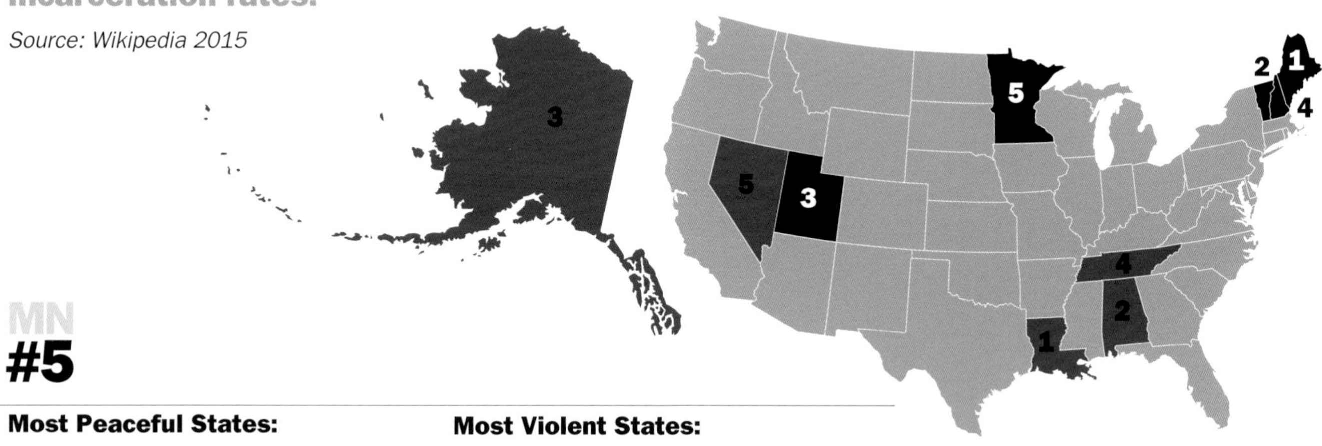

MN
#5

Most Peaceful States:

1. Maine
2. Vermont
3. Utah
4. New Hampshire
5. **Minnesota**

Source: WalletHub 2016

Most Violent States:

1. Louisiana
2. Alabama
3. Alaska
4. Tennessee
5. Nevada

© Mirko Vitali/Dreamstime

Leader in Reducing Recidivism

Twin Cities Rise is a successful antipoverty training program that empowers mostly minority men and women who have had serious trauma in their families and lives, particularly in prison.

Through this program, prison recidivism has been reduced by 50% and, on average, a graduate goes from earning $5,000 to $27,000 annually. Job retention is 80%, twice the national average. The personal empowerment program has become a national model.

Chapter 6.
All the children actually are above average.

Hennepin County Library

A national leader, Hennepin County Library is, on a per-capita basis,
#1 in computer terminals
#2 in capital spending
#3 in operating spending
#3 in number of books
#5 in number of borrowers
#7 in number of visitors
#4 in number of branches

© Dan Anderson

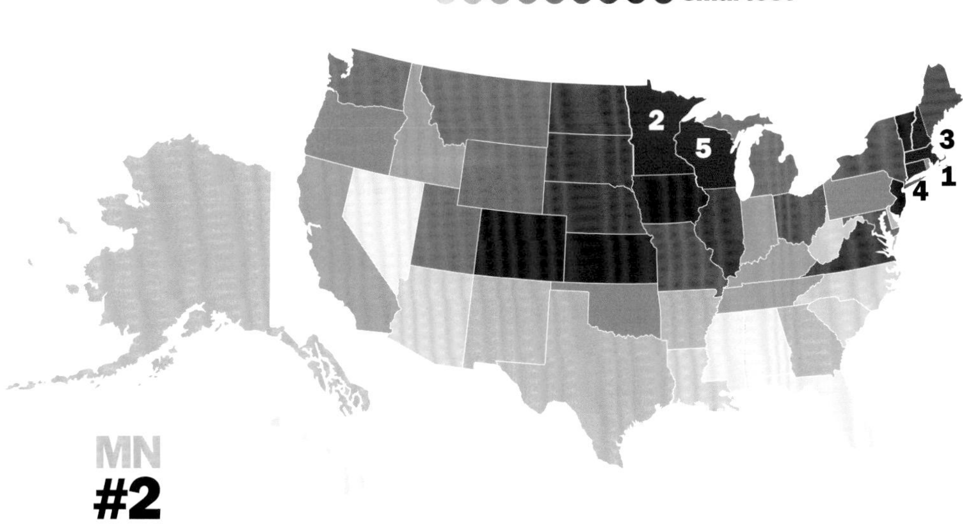

MN
#2

Smartest States:

1. Massachusetts
2. **Minnesota**
3. New Hampshire
4. Connecticut
5. Wisconsin

Source: washingtonpost.com 11/13/15

Minnesota Named Second-Smartest State, behind Massachusetts

A recent CNBC study looked at each state's education system, number of degree-granting institutions, average high school test scores, and elementary school math and reading rankings.

MN
#1

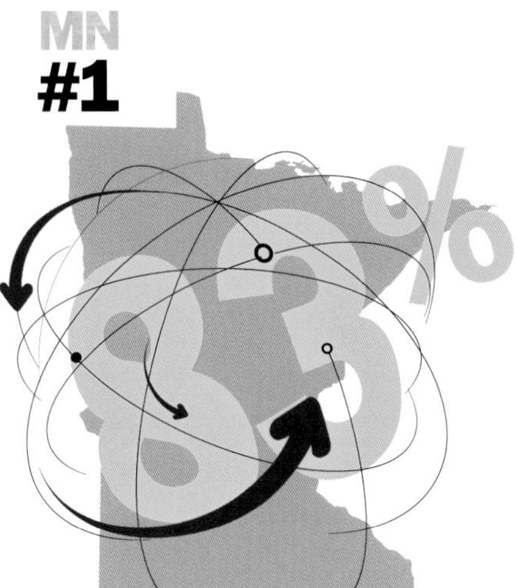

According to *Entrepreneur Magazine*, 83%, or 4.3 million households, use the Internet in Minnesota.

With Bob Dylan's 2016 Nobel Prize for Literature, Minnesota has received 20% of the nation's Nobel Awards for Literature.

MN FACT

The largest number of library transactions in the U.S., and maybe in the world, takes place at the University of Minnesota, which housed for many years, among other collections, the scientific papers of Jane Goodall's chimpanzee research in Tanzania.

The University of Minnesota is the fourth-largest single research campus university (not including any online for-profit schools).

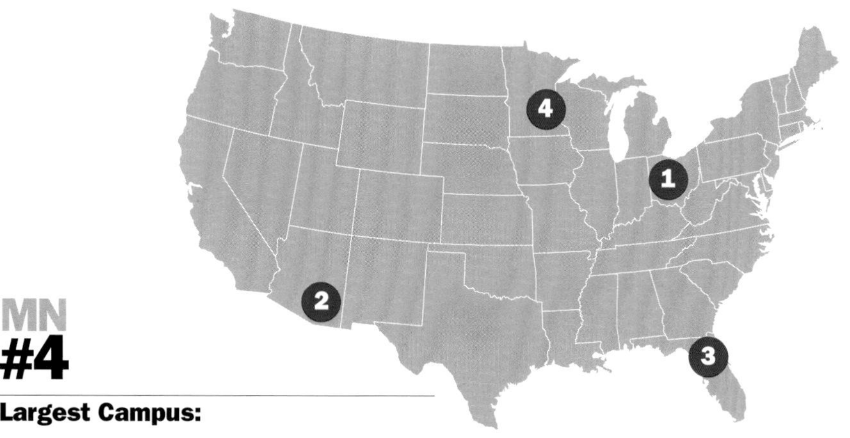

MN
#4

Largest Campus:

1. Ohio State
2. University of Arizona
3. University of Florida
4. **University of Minnesota**

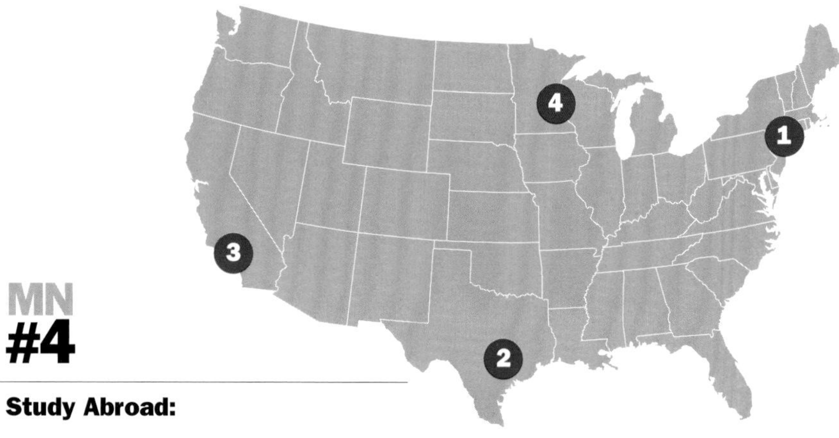

MN
#4

Study Abroad:

1. NYU, New York City
2. University of Texas, Austin
3. USC, Los Angeles
4. **University of Minnesota**

Source: iie.org/research-and-publications/open-doors/data

The importance of education in Minnesota was no doubt the product of our Scandinavian and German ancestors. In 1862 the designation of the state's first Land Grant University had a far-reaching effect. Because of the state's geographic isolation, the University of Minnesota became a magnet for the surrounding region. As it grew in prominence it began to attract students from around the world. Many who come to study here end up staying. The U of M system has approximately 53,000 graduate and undergraduate students enrolled.

#1 Smart Money Management

The U of M ranked #1 for endowment investment returns in 2015, up from #4 in 2014.

400,000

The State University system has 400,000 credit and non-credit students.

top 25

Top 25 Best Public Colleges

Forbes Magazine annually ranks the best U.S. public colleges. The U of M was not only cited as one of the best in the country but also noted for its more than 300 exchange programs around the world. The U's alumni have founded more than 10,000 businesses in Minnesota.

Awards of Excellence

The U of M has won 86 Guggenheim Fellowships and 26 Nobel Prizes.

top 25

The University of Minnesota Law School is in the top 25 nationally.

#8 of 270

The U of M Humphrey School of Public Policy is ranked #8 out of 270 schools.

Source: U.S. News & World Report

The U of M Humphrey School is #2 in nonprofit management.

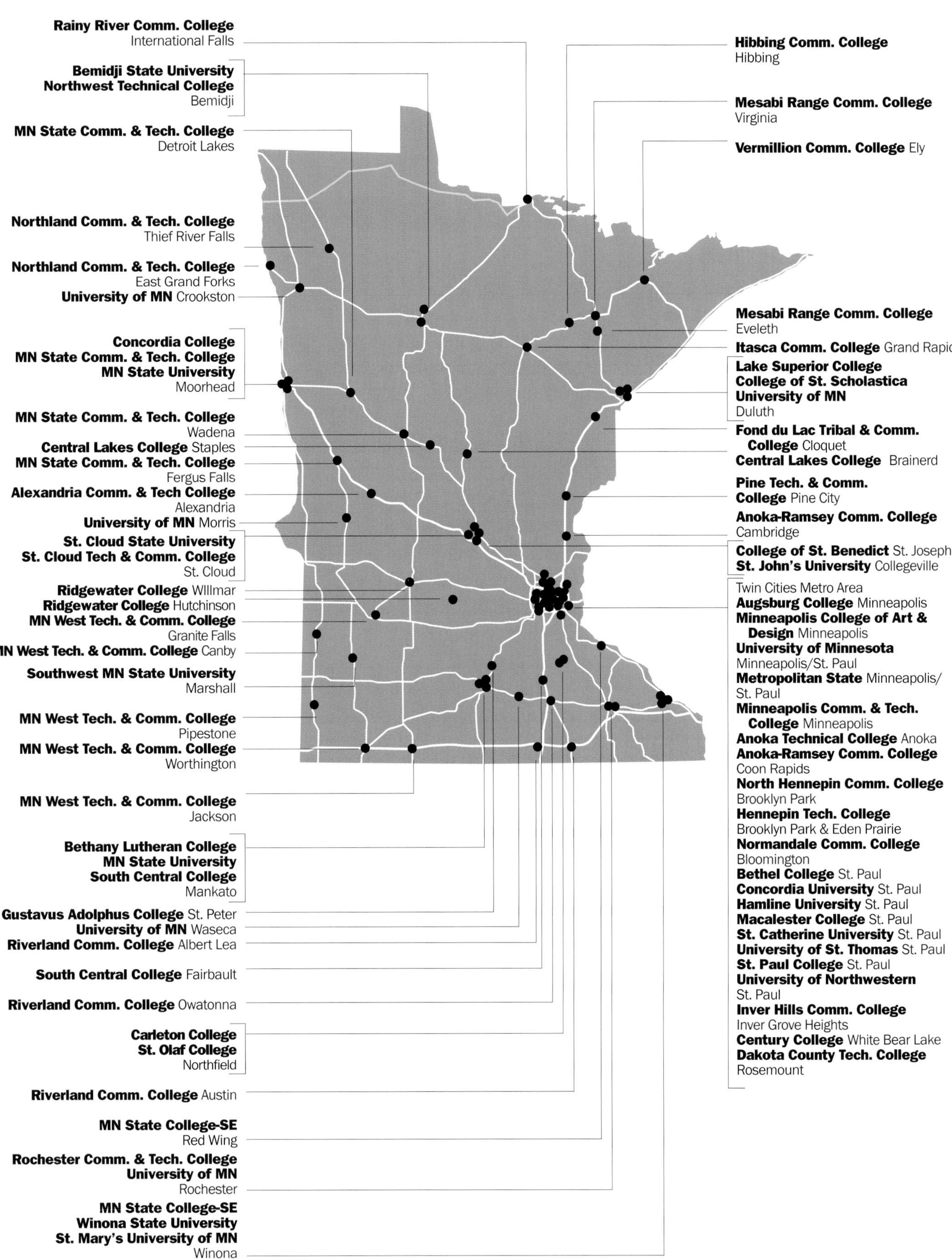

Major Colleges & Universities

In 1963 the state legislature decided that a statewide college system should conveniently service the citizens of rural Minnesota and planned to have a college within 35 miles of most citizens. This proliferation was expensive and ultimately decreased the state's contribution to the main university system.

Carleton

Carleton College in Northfield is in the **top 25 best private colleges** in nation.

© Andrea Rugg

The MacPhail Center for Music, founded in 1907 by a member of the famous Minnesota Orchestra, now serves more than 15,500 students, ranging in age from six weeks to over 100, in music and music therapy. It was one of the first to introduce the Suzuki method in teaching children.

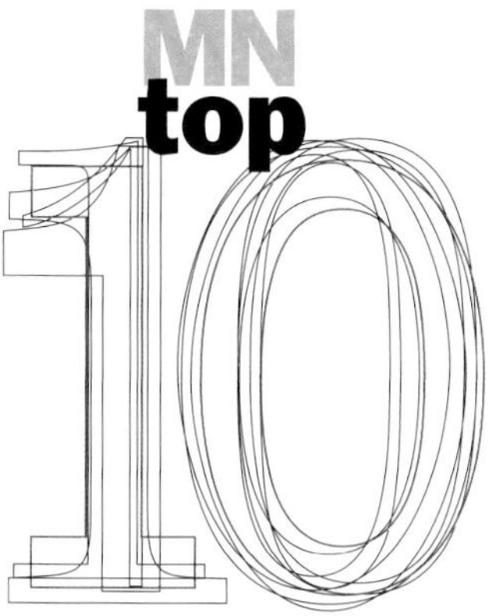

The 125-year-old Minneapolis College of Art and Design (MCAD) is considered to be in the top 10 art colleges in America and was an early adapter in the use of computers in design.

Intense Metro Concentration

When you combine the University of Minnesota's population with that of the other major colleges and universities in the surrounding area (such as the University of St. Thomas, Macalester, Hamline, St. Catherine, St. Olaf, Carleton, and Metro State), the total number of people in the higher education enterprise in the metro area has an enormous impact on the intellectual life of a relatively small city. Few places in the U.S. have such a high ratio of academics to the general population. The Boston area has 150,000 vs. the Twin Cities at 200,000.

Minnesota has three medical schools and three law schools.

summa cum laude

sumo cum laude

Sumo: @ James Salmon 123rf/Dreamstime

According to the Center for Applied Linguistics, Minnesota ranks fourth in language immersion programs, behind Louisiana (French), Hawaii (Hawaiian), and Oregon. Minnesota is also fourth in the nation for percent of population with a high school diploma.

3

4

1

MN

#4

Top Language Immersion Programs:

1. Louisiana (French)
2. Hawaii (Hawaiian)
3. Oregon
4. **Minnesota**

First Charter School in U.S.

The first charter school was established in Minnesota in 1992. The state now has 150 charter schools serving more than 48,000 K–12 students.

Leader in the International Baccalaureate Diploma Program

The IB program is offered in 21 Minnesota high schools, allowing students to get a jumpstart by earning college credits while in high school.

The Children Are "All Above Average"
For nine years in a row Minnesota has placed **#1 in ACT scores**. Seniors had an average ACT of 22.9, compared to the nationwide average of 21.

Source: education.state.mn.us/MDE

© University of Minnesota

Minnesota Lags Nationally in Graduation Rates for Students of Color. We Can and Must Do Better.
Fewer than 60% of the state's black and Hispanic students graduate in four years, according to MPR news analysis, ranking Minnesota close to the bottom.

History a Big Hit in High Schools
More than 1,000 junior and senior high school students gather for History Day at the University of Minnesota, making it the largest History Day gathering in the nation.

© Kalmutsuy/Shutterstock

A Very Literate City

Minneapolis has top ranking as the most literate city in the nation, while St. Paul is #4, just behind Seattle and Washington, DC. The ranking is based on six key indicators:

- Number of booksellers
- Educational attainment
- Internet resources
- Library resources
- Newspaper circulation
- Periodical publishing resources

No cities in Texas, Illinois, or California made the top 20.

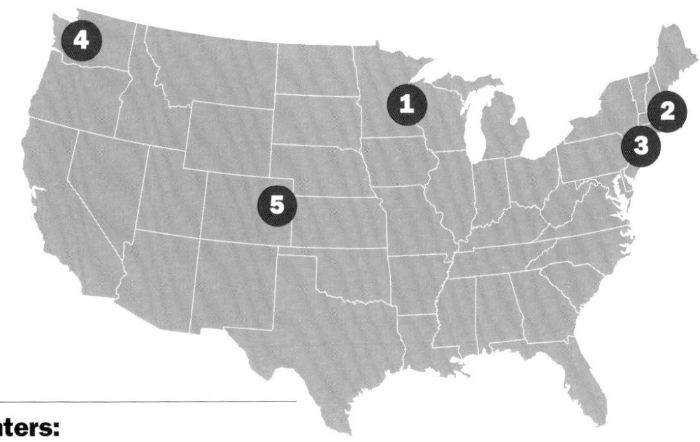

MN
#1

Top Literary Centers:

1. The Loft, Minneapolis
2. GrubStreet, Boston
3. Poets House, NYC
4. Hugo House, Seattle
5. Lighthouse, Denver

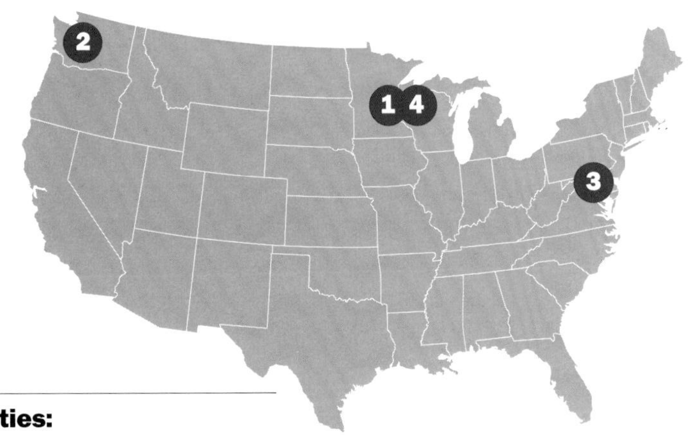

MN
#1&4

Most Literate Cities:

1. Minneapolis
2. Seattle
3. Washington, DC
4. St. Paul

Source: Central Connecticut State Univesity

The Minnesota Reading Corp is the Largest AmeriCorps Tutoring Program in the U.S.

The Minnesota Reading Corps began in 2003 and today has 1,574 AmeriCorps members reaching 30,000 disadvantaged children.

In the Land of the Book People

"At the first dinner party my wife and I attended after moving to Minneapolis in 1974, our host asked the guests around the table to tell about the latest book they were reading. Not stories of business triumphs or tragedies, family calamities or celebrations, not celebrity gossip, but what one had learned from the breadth and depth only books can offer. Ka-boom, went my trembling heart. I joined a book club.

The Loft Literary Center was founded above a small bookstore in Minneapolis in 1975. Today it is the largest literary services organization in the country. As I say, Book People.

In 1985, a sign went up on a nineteenth-century warehouse a block down Third Street from my office: Minnesota Center for Book Arts (MCBA). Walking through that door felt like discovering Gina Lollobrigida, Sophia Loren, and Marcello Mastroianni in mad embrace. Sophia was setting lead type in a printer's apron. Gina was crafting handmade paper for the trade. Marcello was cutting blocks for six-color wood engravings. I was in love among the Book People.

In 2000, Open Book opened its doors at 1011 Washington Avenue South in three revitalized nineteenth-century storefronts as a permanent home for The Loft, MCBA and Milkweed Editions, a non-profit literary press, as a center for book lovers. The Loft offers classes on how to craft a poem, story, novel, screenplay or blog post; MCBA teaches typesetting, bookbinding, book design, printing, papermaking and more. Milkweed Editions publishes beautifully written, edited, and designed books, one of the three major nonprofit literary publishers that call Minnesota home (the others: Graywolf Press and Coffee House Press).

Open Book has been visited by cultural emissaries from around the world, wondering how they too could build a comprehensive center for literary life. But what could be more important than crafting, printing, and publishing a sequence of sound and sense to last ten thousand years?

Minnesota is a cultural mecca, Paris on the Prairie I call it. Don't take my word for it. Open the doors of Open Book and open your ears. Then join a book club. Then write a book."

James P. Lenfestey

Reader, Writer and Lover of Books

© Larry Marcus

Minnesota's culture of volunteering was noted during the American Civil War. When President Lincoln called for volunteers, the 1st Minnesota regiment of 25,000 men was the first to volunteer. On the second day of the battle of Gettysburg, the 1st Minnesota suffered the highest casualty rate per capita of any battle in the Civil War.

Chapter 7. The Emerald City.

Public Domain

$4 Million a Week

Target, the nation's second-largest retailer, not only gives $4 million per week back to the community but also uses its generosity in its marketing mix. People are frequently reminded of their gift and tend to like Target because of it.

Minnesotans and Twin Citians are a generous lot. They give of their money, both individually and corporately, as well as their time. They even give their body parts: Minnesotans are **#1 in the nation for organ donations.**

Glowing Emerald

For decades much has been written about the nonprofit and philanthropic nature of Minnesota. Even the venerable *New York Times* once referred to Minneapolis as "The Emerald City of Giving."

Over a million Minnesotans annually volunteer their time at a rate of 40.4 hours per capita; 34% of those over 16 years of age and almost half of those 65 to 74 years old volunteer regularly. This represents roughly $3.9 billion in services contributed to the nonprofit sector. Reflective of this generous nature is the fact that 70% of Minnesota residents engage in "informal volunteering" like doing favors for neighbors.

Source: Corp for National and Community Services

70%

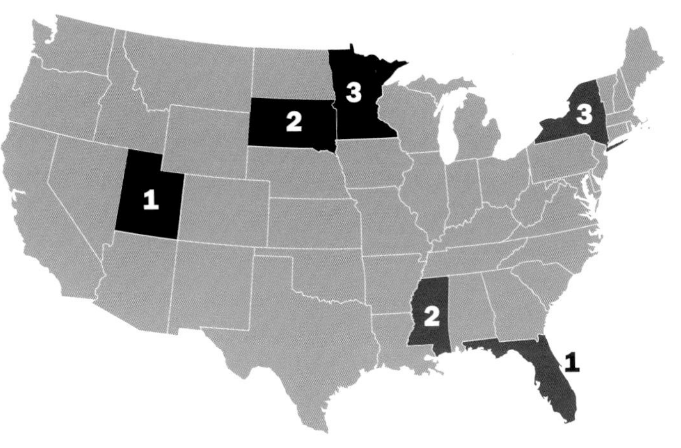

MN
#3

2015 Most Volunteers:

1. Utah – 39.3%
2. South Dakota – 36.8%
3. **Minnesota – 36.3%**

2015 Least Volunteers:

1. Florida – 18.3%
2. Mississippi – 18.4%
3. New York – 19.8%

Source: U.S. Census Bureau/ MN Compass

5&2%

In 1976 the Minneapolis Chamber of Commerce, at the urging of several civic-minded CEOs, created a unique club, the 5% Club (later renamed the Keystone Program), for companies that would commit 5% of their pretax profits to charitable purposes —an astounding sum, considering the pressure on public companies to deliver everything to their bottom line. Subsequently, a 2% Club was created for those companies that couldn't quite commit to giving 5%.

There are 1,450 registered charitable foundations in the state. On an annual basis in Minnesota, 47% of charitable giving is derived from the large number of corporate foundations or charitable giving programs in the state, including the Target Corporation and the General Mills Foundation. Private family and independent foundations represent 36% of the giving, while community foundations, including the Minneapolis, St. Paul, and Women's Foundations, are 17% of the total charitable grants in the state. (These proportions are likely to change dramatically as the Margaret A. Cargill Foundation gears up.)

47%
36%
17%

$1.3 billion

In 2015 charitable giving in Minnesota was up 8% over 2014 as the top 50 foundations and corporations gave away $1.3 billion. Giving increased again in 2016.

#25

Founded in 1915, the Minneapolis Foundation is one of the oldest community foundations in the U.S. It currently ranks 25th in assets. Similarly, The Women's Foundation of Minnesota, created in 1983, was the first private foundation in the nation dedicated solely to equality for women and girls.

11½%

49,926

Nonprofit organizations play a critical role in the quality of life in Minnesota—providing for social services, education, health care, and the arts, and employing a significant number of local residents. Including hospitals and higher education institutions, nonprofits comprise 11.5% of the workforce in the state. Minnesota ranks ninth in the nation in nonprofit employment. Currently, there are 49,926 nonprofits registered in the state.

Courtesy of Union University

$13 million

The Page Foundation

Alan Page, an NFL Hall of Fame tackle and former justice of the Minnesota Supreme Court, founded a nonprofit organization in 1988 to encourage students of color facing incredible barriers to attain their educational dreams. Since then they have granted over $13 million. In 2015 and 2016, 536 Page Scholars will be awarded $900,000 in grants.

#5

$71,008

Some contend that generosity in the Twin Cities is due in part to its high household income ($71,800, fifth highest in the nation) and low cost of living.

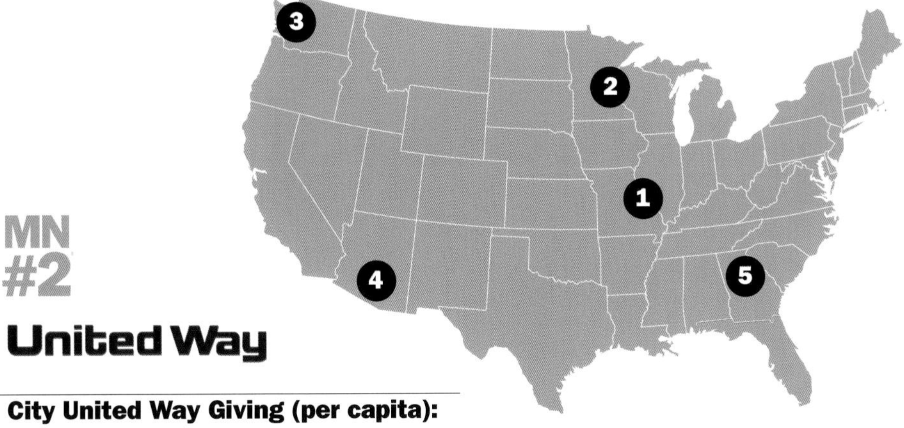

MN
#2

United Way

City United Way Giving (per capita):

1. St. Louis – $29.45
2. **Twin Cities – $29.12**
3. Seattle – $19.95
4. Phoenix – $19.78
5. Atlanta – $18.05

Popular Senators

Minnesotans seem to love their two U.S. Senators, as does the nation. Senator Amy Klobuchar and Al Franken were recently ranked in the top 10 of the U.S. Senate. Only Maine and Minnesota had two on that list.

© Craig Lassig, Associated Press

Citizenship

Civic participation seems to go hand in hand with an informed and generous population. Among the many active citizen's groups in Minnesota, three are especially worth noting. The Citizens League, founded in the Twin Cities in 1952, is a good-government advocacy and policy group that brings together a large number of citizens to study the state's and region's most compelling problems—infrastructure needs, taxes, and water quality, for example.

Minnesota houses two major and opposing public policy think tanks: the conservative Center of the American Experiment and the progressive research and advocacy organization Growth and Justice.

Given this level of engagement, it is understandable that Minnesota ranks #1 in the nation in voter turnout.

MN
#1

Highest Election Turnout 2016

1. Minnesota – 74.5%
2. Wisconsin – 73.0%
3. Maine – 70.8%
4. New Hampshire – 69.8%

Lowest Election Turnout

1. Hawaii – 44.5%
2. West Virginia – 46.8%
3. Oklahoma – 49.6%
4. Texas – 50.1%

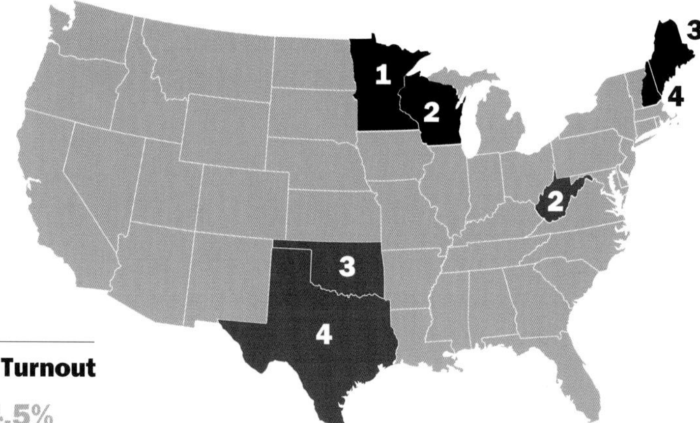

2nd for youth turnout in 2012

3rd most politically engaged

Source: wallethub.com

© Dreamstime

MN FACT

Four Minnesotans have run for president of the U.S.

1. Harold Stassen: 1944, 1948, 1952, 1964, 1968, 1980, 1984, 1988, and 1992
2. Eugene McCarthy: 1968, 1972, and 1976
3. Hubert Humphrey: 1960 and 1964
4. Walter Mondale: 1984

Public Domain

Courtesy National Archives & Records

Public Domain

Public Domain

MN FACT

A Minnesotan has run for president of the U.S. in 55 of the past 72 years.

Vice President Mondale was recently described by the Academy of Political Science as America's **best vice president**, changing the role of the office for decades to come.

"I love Minnesota. I think most of us do. Our state is at the very top. It's an amazing state. We have the best economy. Our schools are at the top. Our public service here is amazing. Our ethics here is amazing. We are an honest state. No statewide constitutional elected officer has ever been indicted or convicted in the last fifty years or longer. I can't think of any other state that even comes close. Our politics are open and honest. While we suffer from the harsh differences reflective of our national politics, we have less of it and I think most of us are trying to keep an open and positive system because it is who we are."

Walter F. Mondale

Former United States Vice President

MN FACT

No one can recall any Minnesota constitutional elected state officer or member of congress ever having been indicted or convicted of a crime. No other state can make that claim.

© Dan Anderson

MINNESOTA

Media

Newspapers have been part of the Twin Cities' community infrastructure since their early days. The *Minnesota Pioneer* was founded in St. Paul in 1849, and the *Minneapolis Tribune* was established in 1867. The Twin Cities now are headquarters to two Pulitzer Prize–winning newspapers, the *Star Tribune* and the *Pioneer Press.*

MINN POST

In addition, the state is one of the first in the nation to have a daily online news source, *MinnPost*, which covers public policy issues of importance to Minnesotans without having to cover crime, crashes, or catastrophes. 450,000 people visit *MinnPost* weekly, and 100,000 are frequent readers.

Twin Cities Public Television (TPT)

TPT is known as one of the preeminent PBS affiliate stations in the country, both for producing and broadcasting public media programming in the region and for national broadcast. Operating on multiple broadcast frequencies and online, TPT is **the most highly viewed PBS station per capita in the country.** Begun in 1957, TPT currently operates with an annual budget of $28 million.

A Giant News Source
American Public Media (parent to Minnesota Public Radio and Southern California Public Radio) is the largest station-based public radio system in the nation. It operates stations, creates national content, and distributes programming virtually everywhere in the U.S. *A Prairie Home Companion, The Splendid Table, Marketplace,* and the *BBC World Service* are some of the many programs that reach 19 million listeners weekly.

Minnesota Public Radio
A giant in itself, Minnesota Public Radio distributes programming through 45 network stations and 39 signal translators throughout the state and parts of surrounding states. MPR reaches 900,000 people each week and has won more than 1,000 awards for excellence in programming. MPR is **the only public station system in the nation to broadcast to 100% of a state's population.**

With an operating budget of $91 million, MPR and its parent, American Public Radio, have **a budget that is second only to that of National Public Radio.** Even more remarkable is that 64% of MPR's income comes from the public. MPR can be heard in the Twin Cities on 91.1 FM News, 99.5 FM Classical Music (the largest producer and distributor of classical music programming in the country), and 89.3 FM The Current (playing new music seldom heard on commercial stations).

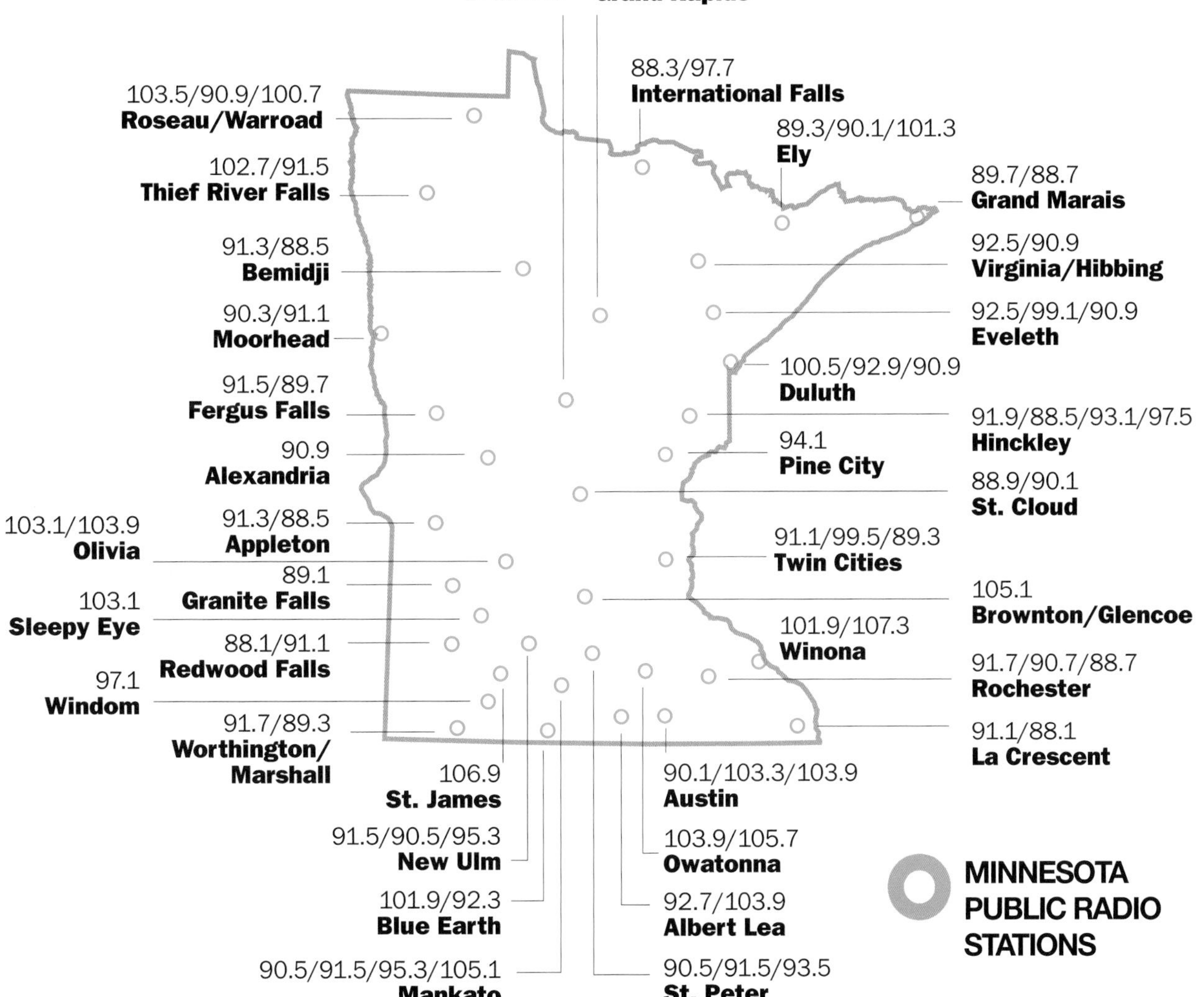

MN FACT

A Prairie Home Companion **airs on 672 public radio stations as well as American Armed Forces Radio. The Fitzgerald Theater in St. Paul, where Garrison Keillor and the new host Chris Thile perform, is owned by American Public Radio.**

© Prairie Home Productions

AM~FM
KSJN

Chapter 8.

Don't tax you, don't tax me, tax the man behind the tree.

Factors

Some people wonder how a demographically small, cold, and high-tax state, isolated in the dead center of North America, could have such a vibrant economy. Seven factors are partial answers to that question.

Economic Diversity

Minnesota's success is not, as in most states, dependent on one or two industries but rather is led by several business segments. A balanced economy has kept Minnesota's unemployment rate near the national bottom in good times and bad.

Other Services
Government
Farming
Mining & Logging
Construction
Manufacturing
Trade, Transportation, & Utilities
Information
Financial Activities
Professional & Business Services
Education & Health Care
Leisure & Hospitality

Well-Educated Workforce

Minnesota is home to a great university and 74 other colleges and universities. The Twin Cities are in the top five cities with the most college students in residence and is #1 on a per-capita basis. Minnesota has the second-highest percentage of students completing high school in the nation. Minnesota students rank #1 in ACT scores, and over one-third of high school graduates in the state earn college degrees.

An Unusually High Quality of Life

Due to an early and continued investment in the arts, entertainment, and the outdoors.

Effective, Honest, & Progressive Government

A Cherished Environment
Clean air, abundant water, and preserved wildernesses.

An Inspired Work Ethic & Generosity
Stemming from its early Northern European settlers' belief in hard work and giving back.

Worldwide Transportation Options
Rail, road, or water plus one-stop air routes to Asia and Europe.

Where Minnesota Ranks for Business

A comprehensive analysis by CNBC ranked Minnesota #1 in 2015 and #4 in 2016 for business climate based on these 10 factors. Total possible points appear in black, Minnesota ranking in red.

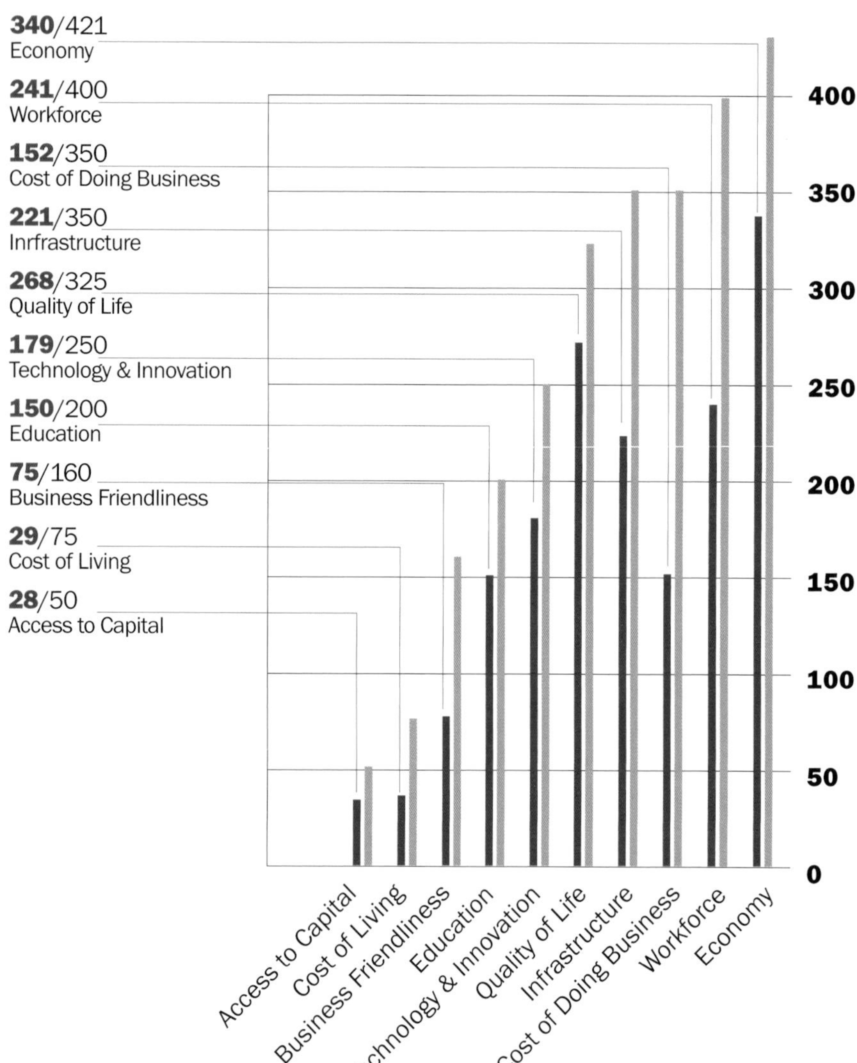

MN
#5 & #2 & #34

Forbes

Forbes magazine ranked Minnesota #5 for economic climate, #2 for quality of life, and #34 for taxes and business cost.

U.S. News & World Report ranks MN the third-best state overall. Good schools, access to great health care, low cost of living, and high median household income were primary factors. Minnesota ranked #2 for economic advancement and employment opportunities.

Source: U.S. News & World Report, *3/2/17*

MN
#3

***U.S. News & World Report* Best States:**

1. Massachusetts
2. New Hampshire
3. **Minnesota**

MN FACT

The Minneapolis–St. Paul International Airport (MSP) ranked fifth best in the world in 2016 for on-time flights. Tokyo's Haneda Airport was #1 for on-time.

MN #1&5

MSP ranked third best in the nation in transit time to downtown Minneapolis from the airport at approximately 30 minutes.

Source: FiveThirtyEight's Nate Silver

© Tony Webster

Google

amazon

MN
#1

3M Tops for Millennials

Topping such brand and corporate names as Google, Apple, and Amazon, 3M was the most appealing company for 15-to-35-year-old workers, according to a survey of high-achieving Millennials.

Source: StarTribune *6/15/16*

3M

Minnesota is at the forefront of the new "circular economy." Committed to trying to reuse everything, 3M, Cargill, Target, General Mills, and other top Minnesota companies are buying into the concept. One company can't do it alone, but a dedicated consortium of companies can make real progress toward a "no waste" goal.

MN FACT

The Better Business Bureau was founded in Minnesota.

TAYLOR

Minnesota's Top Eight Private Companies:

1. Cargill – $120.4 billion
2. Carlson Companies – $4.6 billion
3. Mortenson Construction – $3.7 billion
4. Holiday Companies – $3.2 billion
5. Rosen's Diversified – $3.2 billion
6. Schwans Food Company – $3 billion
7. Andersen Windows – $2.4 billion
8. Taylor Corporation – $2 billion

#14, $130 billion

#36, $74.5 billion

#69, $42.6 billion

#72, $41.9 billion

#98, $31.8 billion

#138, $21.3 billion

#164, $18.3 billion

#171, $17.9 billion

#203, $15.2 billion

#213, $14.2 billion

C.H. ROBINSON

#225, $13.4 billion

#247, $12.2 billion

#255, $11.6 billion

#310, $9.3 billion

#320, $9 billion

#333, $8.5 billion

FORTUNE 500

Minnesota ranks third, behind the District of Columbia and Connecticut, in number of Fortune 500 companies per capita in the state. Rather than having concentration in a few industries, Minnesota's Fortune 500 companies span 15 different industries.

Source: www.ceo.com/entrepreneurial

Great Old Names in Minnesota Business

Hill: railroad
Pillsbury: milling
Weyerhaeuser: lumber
MacMillan: commodities
Carlson: hotels
Bell: milling
Cargill: commodities
McKnight: manufacturing
Congdon: mining

Cargill

Cargill, with over $120 billion in revenue and 153,000 employees, is based in Minnesota. It has been ranked as the largest privately held company for 28 of the past 30 years. Koch Industries, Dell, Bechtel, and PriceWaterhouse, all located elsewhere, follow Cargill in size.

© Cade E. Smith

MN FACT

Cargill is a world leader in salt production.

© Kevin, Alameda, CA, https://commons.wikimedia.org

Salt Box: © Braniffman/Dreamstime

MN FACT

An Unusual Business Diversification

For the past 40 years, ALVIN, a mini-submarine, has explored the ocean's depths. Admiral Hyman Rickover didn't want major shipbuilders to divert energy and money away from space projects. So as not to annoy the good admiral, they didn't bid on building the mini-sub. None other than cereal maker General Mills built it.

Minnesota's economic climate has been a major factor in the number of medium-sized companies based here that have grown into giants. Management talent tends to stay. The Twin Cities have the lowest out-migration of corporate professionals of any of the 22 largest metropolitan areas.

Source: Star Tribune *4/19/15*

#4 3M
#42 Medtronic

The Boston Consulting Group ranks 3M #4 and Medtronic #42 as the most innovative companies in the world.

Minnesota is the fourth-best place for female entrepreneurs.

New and small businesses in the state were ranked #5 in national survival rates between 2009 and 2014.

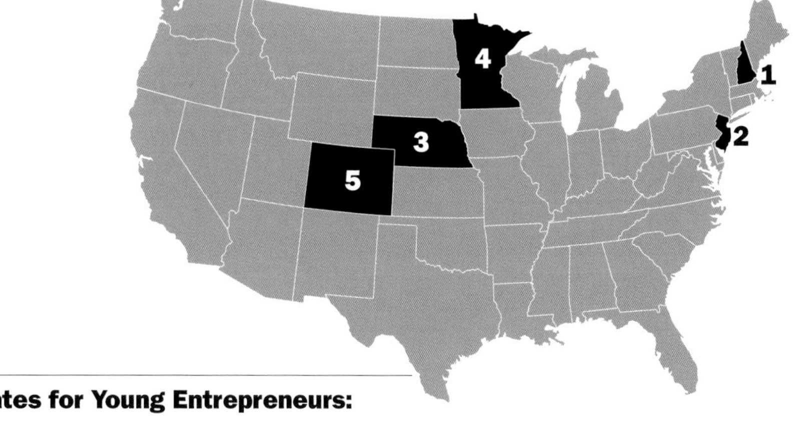

MN #4

Top States for Young Entrepreneurs:

1. New Hampshire
2. New Jersey
3. Nebraska
4. **Minnesota**
5. Colorado

Source: NerdWallet

© Diego Rivera/Detroit Institute of Arts

7,400= 13%

Minnesota is home to 7,400 manufacturers, representing 13% of the jobs in the state. With 193,700 jobs in manufacturing, the Twin Cities rank seventh in the nation according to the U.S. Bureau of Labor Statistics.

$1,000,000.00

Minnesota ranks 14th in number of millionaire households on a per-capita basis.

The Financial & Professional Services Economy

Minnesota is headquarters to the Ninth Federal Reserve and home to the nation's fifth-largest bank, US Bank, as well as an unusually high number of wealth management firms, the largest of which is Ameriprise Financial. The Twin Cities rank second in the nation for concentration of financial services.

MN #7 MILKEN INSTITUTE

Minnesota ranks seventh nationally for its technology and science business prowess, according to Milken Institute's State Technology and Science Index 2016.

MN #6

Salary increases in the technology sector have recently boosted the state's average household income, which is already sixth highest in the nation at $63,488 vs. $56,516 for the national average.

#5

Twin Cities median household income ranks fifth nationally at $71,008.

Source: mncompass.org/economy

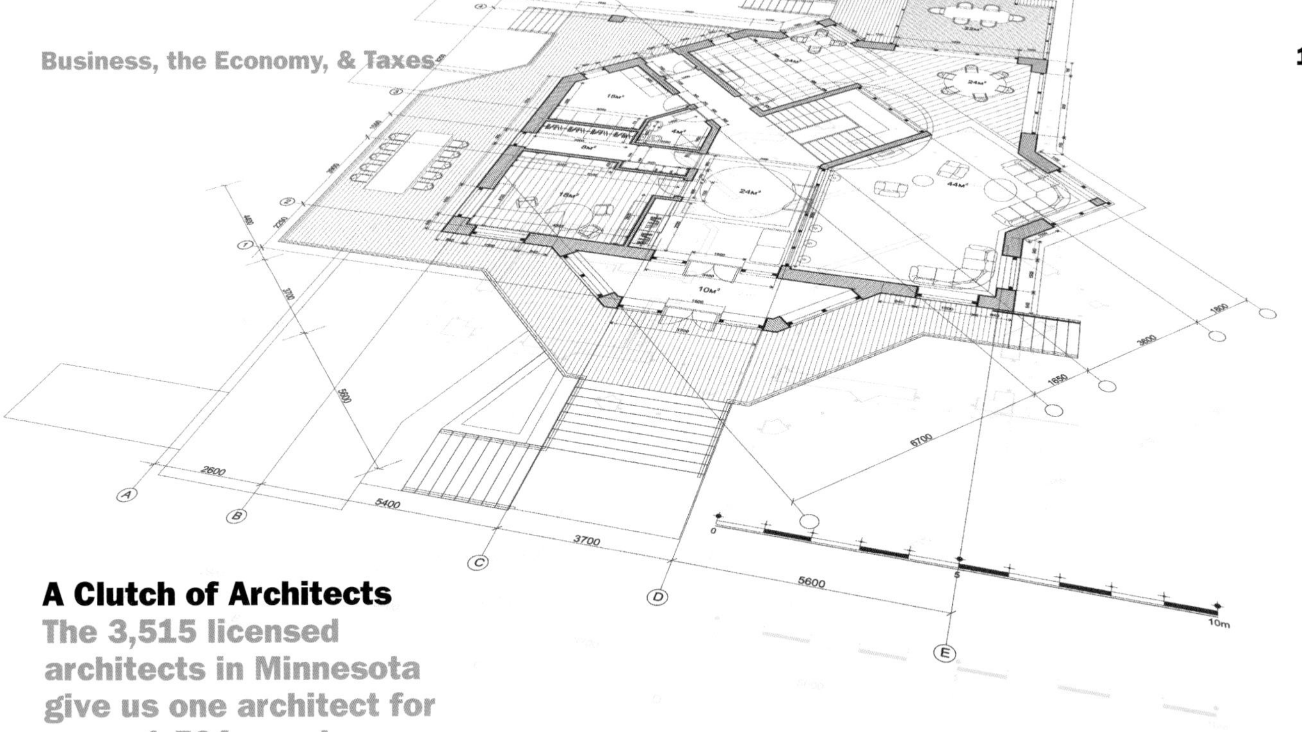

A Clutch of Architects

The 3,515 licensed architects in Minnesota give us one architect for every 1,564 people, the highest per-capita density in America, according to Peter Kramer of Roark, Kramer Kosowski Design.

The Short End of the Federal Stick

Minnesota gets only 54¢ back on every dollar sent to the U.S. government. Very few military contractors are housed in the state. However, Minnesota is #3 in per-capita federal tax payments due to the high median household income. Washington, DC, is #1.

Minnesotans have the highest average credit score at 704 vs. 669 on a national average.

© Bennyartist, rsooll/Shutterstock

© FICO

© Eric Ian

© Sandro

The Twin Cities have always had a large graphic and advertising presence. But in the early 1980s the Twin Cities became dominant in major award shows for advertising creativity. Clients from all over the nation moved their business to a handful of highly creative agencies—clients such as BMW, Arby's, Hertz, Harley-Davidson, H&R Block, Porsche, and Subaru, to name a few. More than 2,000 highly paid professionals in advertising and branding firms create a wake of activity in associated specialties such as printing, design, public relations, photography, film, social marketing, and research.

Some Historic Minnesota Brand Characters
Betty Crocker, Target's Bullseye, Great Northern's Rocky, the Pillsbury Doughboy, Jolly Green Giant, Hamm's Beer Bear, and Red Owl.

All brand names & characters are protected by copyright and/or trademark registration.

Betty Crocker and Pillsbury Doughboy courtesy of the General Mills Archive

Health Care and Related Industries

Led by Medtronic, the Twin Cities house 400 medical technology companies, the largest concentration of med tech companies in the nation. Minnesota is second only to California in medical technology employment. UnitedHealthcare is the largest health insurance company in the nation. Mayo Clinic was named the #1 hospital in the U.S.

Tourism and Hospitality

With close to 12,000 lakes, Minnesota is also home to the largest area preserved for wilderness recreation in the world, Voyageurs National Park and the Boundary Waters Canoe Area.

40 million people annually visit the Mall of America (MOA). With 500 stores (and expanding), the MOA is the nation's largest mall. It's a must-see for any visitors to Minnesota. More people visit the MOA than the Las Vegas strip and Times Square in NYC. (The MOA does not break out visitors from normal shoppers.)

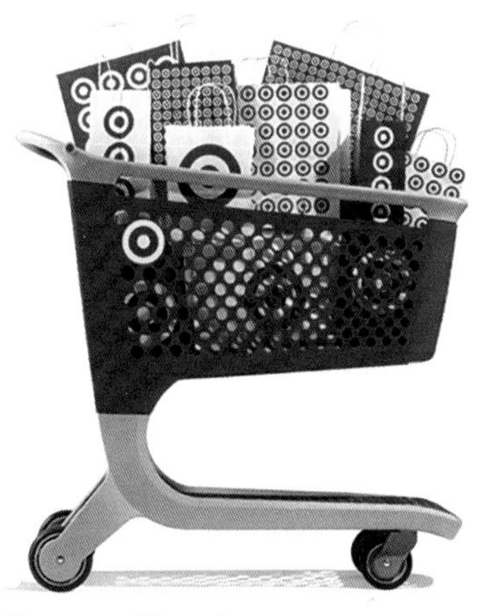

Retail

Target, the nation's #2 retailer (behind Walmart), and Best Buy, the nation's largest electronics retailer, are just two of the many retail brands based in Minnesota. Dairy Queen, Buffalo Wild Wings, Great Clips, and Regis Hair Salons are well-known in their markets.

The Changing Family Farm

Young farmers rarely choose to stay in the farming business. For every two farmers over the age of 65 there is only one under the age of 45. About half of the 74,542 farms in Minnesota are managed by professional farm managers (30 such managers in the state). The land is put into trust and managed by banks or real estate companies.

Agriculture and Food Production

With the massive wheat fields of northwest Minnesota, the rice paddies of central Minnesota, and the richest farmland in the world in south central Minnesota, agriculture and food production have historically been the foundation of the Minnesota economy. Minnesota ranks fifth in gross farm income at $21,699,753. Milling wheels powered by the Mississippi River gave rise to food giants General Mills and Pillsbury. Land O'Lakes, the Schwan Food Company, Hormel, and many other Minnesota food producers market throughout the world.

Minnesota is food self-sufficient, but you might get fat and bored if you only eat what is raised in the state. Minnesota is #1 in growing turkeys, peas, sweet corn, beans, and sugar beets. Yum! You can eat Spam, butter, milk, pizza, eggs, and breakfast cereal, with cake and ice cream as dessert.

Source: USDA Stix service

Infrastructure Condition

Although substantial investment in roads and bridges is needed, the condition of the infrastructure in Minnesota is far better than that of the rest of the nation. Minnesota has 6% of the nation's highways with 50,000 miles (another source said 140,000). Only 9% of the state's bridges are structurally deficient vs. 24% in the U.S. overall. 6.7% of roadways in the state are poor vs. 10.7% nationally.

Source: NerdWallet

© David R. Youngren, Hastings Bridge Watch

Creativity & Innovation

Minnesota ranks 10th in in the nation for patents.

MN

#1

Job Creation:

1. Minnesota

2. Georgia

3. Utah

Source: Gallup/2015

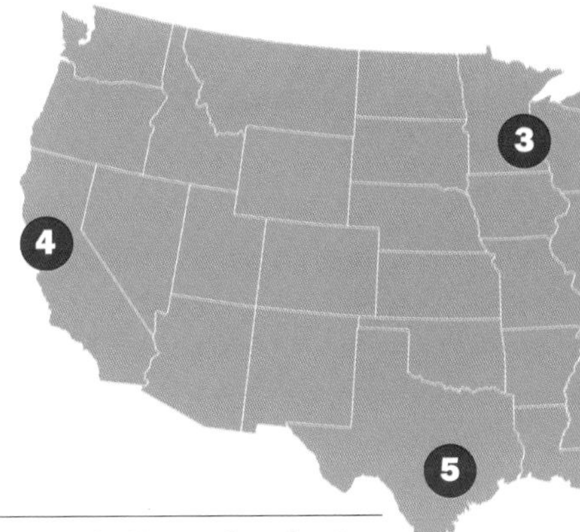

MN

#3

Best Opportunities for College Graduates:

1. Washington, DC

2. Boston

3. Minneapolis

4. San Francisco

5. Austin

Source: investopedia.com/articles/personal finance

Starting a Business

Economic website NerdWallet names the Twin Cities the fourth-best place to start a business. (Part of the ranking was based on having the highest number of businesses per hundred people and low unemployment.)

Significant MN Inventions

The *Harvard Business Review* ranks Minnesota second in innovations. (*Forbes* ranks Minnesota ninth.)

Furnace Thermostat
Developed by Honeywell, a legendary company for innovation.

Masking and Scotch Tape
From 3M, Minnesota's leader in patents (16,000).

Rollerblade
Inline skates designed to work like ice skates without ice.

Climate-Controlled Shopping Centers
The first was built in 1954 in Edina, and the MOA is currently the largest.

The Snowmobile
A great contributor to quality of life for snowbound America.

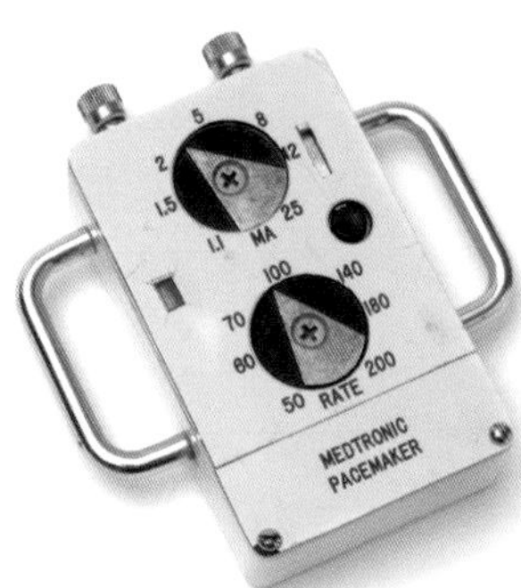

Implantable Pacemaker
The invention that launched Medtronic.

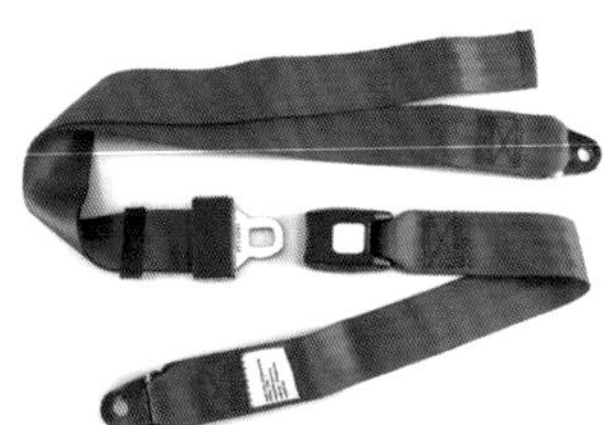

Retractable Seat Belt
Instrumental in saving millions of lives.

Supercomputer
First used to model complex phenomena such as hurricanes and galaxies.

In-Ear Hearing Aid
The first to put transistors into a small plastic shell for the ear.

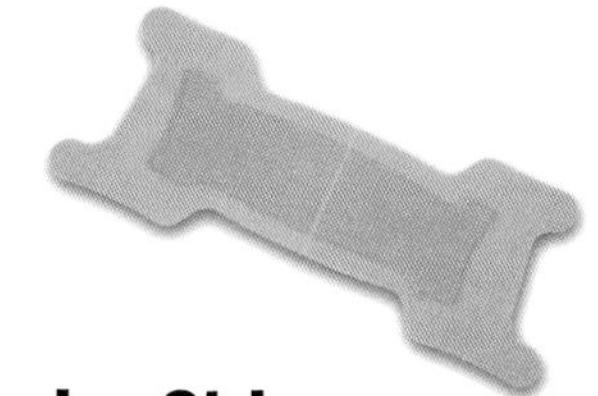

Nasal Adhesive Strip
Breathe Right's strip opens the nasal passage for people having trouble breathing through their noses.

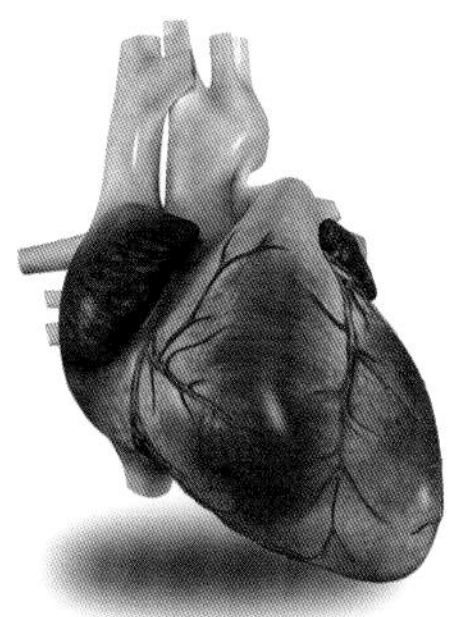

Organ Transplants
Open-heart surgery plus successful pancreas, kidney, and bone marrow transplants were first performed at the University of Minnesota.

Satellite TV Broadcasting
After 13 years in research, Stanley Hubbard developed a satellite that could transmit dozens of channels to an 18-inch satellite dish. The company was sold to DIRECTV.

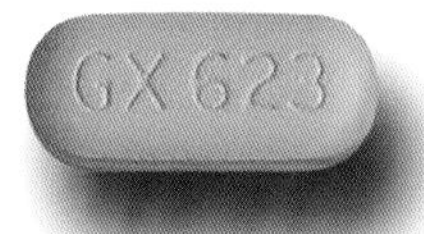

Ziagen
The most lucrative source of licensing income in the University of Minnesota's history. The drug led to a breakthrough in AIDS medications.

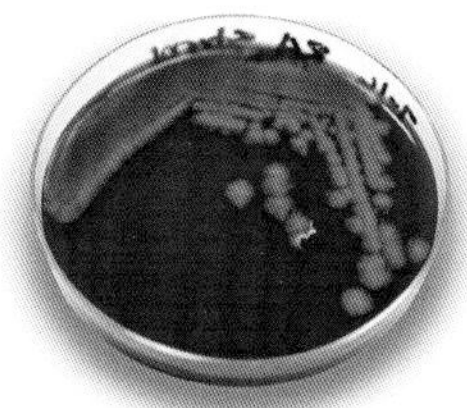

Fast Anthrax Test
It can detect the anthrax bacteria in human and environmental samples in less than an hour.

Tactical Micro-Robot
The Recon Scout is a small, remote-controlled robot that allows military and law enforcement personnel to see into dark and dangerous situations without putting themselves in harm's way.

Prosthetic Heart Valve
A new, durable design and the forerunner of more innovations to come.

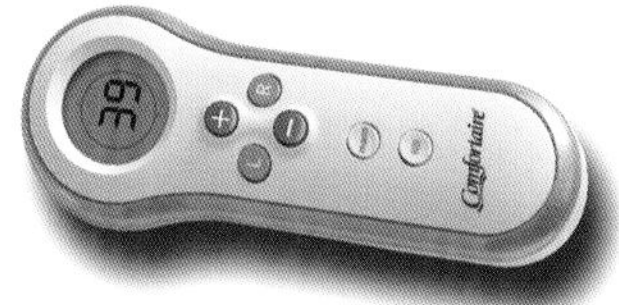

Sleep Number Mattress
Allows the sleeper to adjust the firmness.

Taconite Pellets
Kept Minnesota a world leader in producing iron. The technology allowed mining companies to separate rock from pure iron and turn it into pellets ready for the blast furnaces.

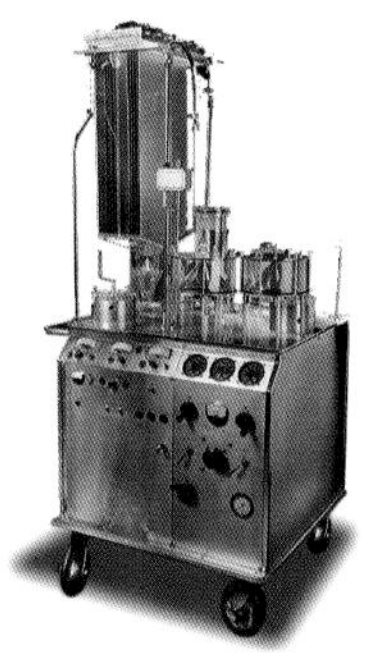

Blood Pump
The device that keeps oxygen pumped into the bloodstream during heart surgery.

Black Box Flight Recorder
Crucial to determining the cause of an airplane crash.

Gallup Economic Confidence

Politics, economics, religion, and other measures of well-being are used to construct Gallup's annual poll, State of the States. Minnesota received the highest economic confidence score in a seven-year trend.

MN
#1

Gallup Economic Confidence:

1. **Minnesota**
2. Maryland
3. California
4. Hawaii
5. Colorado

Financial Savvy

Minnesota is the most financially savvy state, according to an analysis by WalletHub. The consumer website compiled 20 relevant metrics based on spending and debt, financial literacy scores, and credit and savings.

AAA Bond Rating

Minnesota is one of 13 states to receive a triple-A rating for its bonds, thereby saving interest costs for infrastructure borrowing.

© Taiga/Shutterstock

© Shutterstock

MN
#2

USA TODAY
A GANNETT COMPANY

Minnesota Second-Best Run State in America

A 24/7 Wall Street study released on 12/6/16 in *USA Today* ranked Minnesota second-best in the nation. The state was ranked fifth in 2014 and 2015. Included in the ranking criteria were an unemployment rate of 3.5% (tied seventh lowest), credit rating of Aa1/AA+, a poverty rate of 10.2% (tied third lowest), a fourth-lowest uninsured rate of 4.5%, and the sixth-highest median household income.

Unemployment Consistency

In 2015 unemployment was 3.5% in Minnesota, ranking the state seventh in the nation. While the nation's unemployment was in double digits in 2009, Minnesota's was 7.8%. In 2016 the unemployment rate for college graduates was 2.6%.

"We seem to be the last state to go into recession and the first to come out."

Bruce A. Thomson
Minnesota entrepreneur

"It's hard to get talent to come to the Twin Cities, but once they are here it's almost impossible to get them to leave."

Robert Macdonald
Worldwide recruiter for Russell Reynolds executive search firm

© Mega Pixel/Shutterstock

Myles Shaver of the Carlson School of Management said that thousands of highly skilled workers come to Minnesota and want to stay. However when compared to 21 similar cities, the Twin Cities ranked 19th at the rate talent moved here. Once folks are here the situation is reversed. Minnesota had the second-lowest outflow of any state in 2000.

Source: Star Tribune *Sun Apr 9, 2015.)*

© xyzproject/123RF

Don't tax you, don't tax me, tax the man behind the tree!

No one in the history of the world likes to pay taxes. Americans think their founding fathers broke away from England because of high taxes. "Not so!" says Bill Bryson in his book *Made in America*. He contends that the tax rate for the colonists was 50 times smaller than for their English countrymen across the pond. The small tax imposed on the colonists was to provide for their safety. Many of the Stamp Act duties were repealed before they had to be paid.Yet anti-tax fervor had as great an appeal then as it does now.

© xyzproject

Some states "tax the man behind the tree" through taxes on tourists or natural resource extraction.

Minnesota has adopted a progressive tax system that obligates the wealthy to pay high taxes. This, combined with the third-highest business and corporate tax rate, gives Minnesota a "high tax state" reputation. The business and corporate tax is generally reduced through allowable deductions.

Courtesy of MN Historical Society

In 1924 Minnesota's Republican governor Theodore Christianson was among the first, but not the last, candidate to appeal to the voters because of his animosity toward taxes. His campaign slogan was "More Ted, Less Tax." Tightwad Ted was his nickname. Differing tax philosophies have created healthy tensions between Republican and Democratic candidates and voters since that time.

M1 MINNESOTA·REVENUE **Individual Income Tax 2012** 201211

Leave unused boxes blank. Do not use staples on anything you submit.

Please Print

Your First Name and Initial: John
Last Name: Smith
Your Social Security Number: 321654987

Place an X if a Foreign Address:
If a Joint Return, Spouse's First Name and Initial: Maria
Last Name: Smith
Spouse's Social Security Number: 987987987

Current Home Address (Street, Apartment Number, Route): 123 Main st
Place an X if a New Address:
Your Date of Birth (mm/dd/yyyy)

City
State
Zip Code
Spouse's Date of Birth

Filing Status

2012 Federal Filing Status (place an X in one oval box):
(1) Single
(2) Married filing joint
(3) Married filing separate: Enter spouse's name and Social Security number here
(4) Head of household
(5) Qualifying widow(er)

8th highest 9th

Just How High is High?

The Minnesota Center for Fiscal Excellence ranks Minnesota ninth in total tax burden. The Tax Foundation, a more conservative source of tax information, ranks Minnesota eighth highest in the nation in total tax burden.

National average 9.9
Minnesota 10.8
New York, highest at 12.7
Alaska, lowest at 6.5

Form 1040

The Minnesota Estate Tax

In 2015, according to Minnesota Commissioner of Finance, Myron Franz, 800 Minnesota taxpayers had to pay 10 to 16% on the difference between the value of the estate they inherited and their allowable exemptions (after contributions to charity). It is unknown how many people leave Minnesota to avoid the estate tax.

Source: MN Department of Revenue

The Center of the American Experiment, a conservative Minnesota think tank, argues that the tax rate on high-income earners is driving thousands out of the state. Growth and Justice, a progressive think tank, counters by arguing, "If they are really leaving due to higher taxes, they will leave. But their jobs remain." Such arguments have been going on since the time of Tightwad Ted and will undoubtedly continue.

The question for each Minnesotan should be, is the trade-off between quality of life and higher taxes worth it?

Courtesy of Visit St. Paul

Chapter 9. More than lutefisk and lefse.

Annual St. Patrick's Day parade in St. Paul.

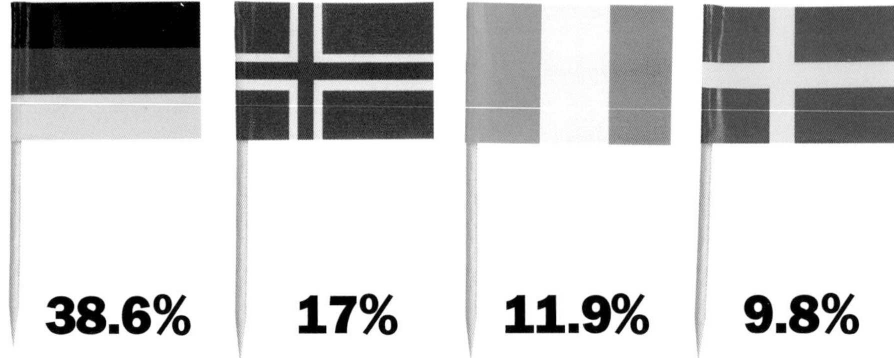

If you asked the average American to describe who Minnesotans are, you would probably get an answer based on years of listening to Garrison Keillor's *A Prairie Home Companion:* basically a bunch of Swedish Lutherans sitting around the kitchen table, eating hotdish and lutefisk. And, of course, this would be followed by "Where the women are strong, the men are good looking, and the children are all above average."

Minnesota has a long history of attracting immigrants to its rich farmlands, forests, mines, and cold climes. Besides the early influx of Scandinavians, Minnesota became a magnet for Germans, Irish, Finns, Poles, Russians, and Eastern Europeans.

Over 75% of Minnesota's residents are of European descent, with the largest reported ancestries being:

German – 38.6%
Norwegian – 17%
Irish – 11.9%
Swedish – 9.8%

The state has had the reputation of being relatively racially homogeneous, but that is changing. The Hispanic population of Minnesota is increasing rapidly, and recent immigrants have come from all over the world, including Hmong, Somalis, Vietnamese, and people of the former Soviet Union.

The tradition of immigration continues today. Minnesota is home to people of many nationalities, partially because of the need and desire of people to escape from war and economic deprivation, and also the presence of many international corporations.

Immigrant Countries in Rank Order

Mexico & Central America
India
Laos
Somalia
Vietnam
Thailand
China
Korea
Ethiopia
Liberia
Tibet
Myanmar

© MN Historical Society

© Hans Slegers/Shutterstock

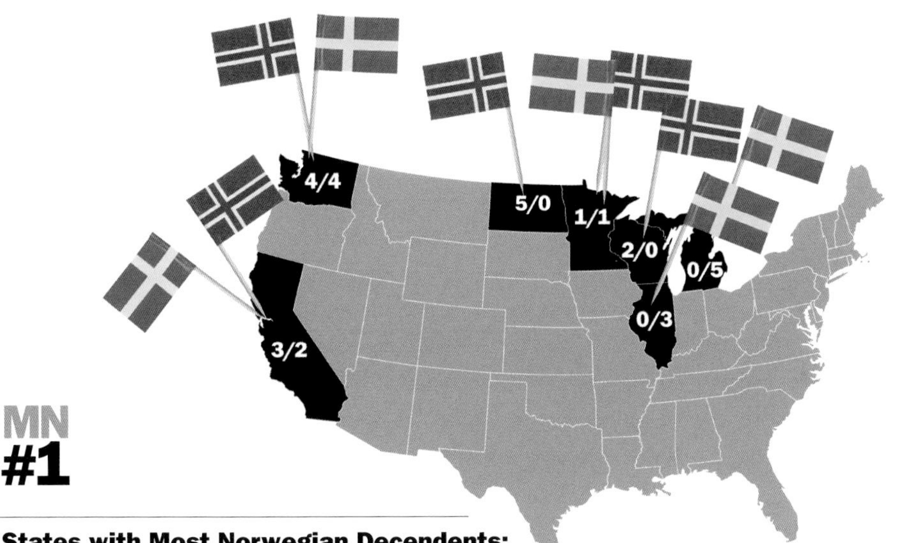

MN
#1

States with Most Norwegian Decendents:

1. **Minnesota**
2. Wisconsin
3. California
4. Washington
5. North Dakota

States with Most Swedish Decendents:

1. **Minnesota**
2. California
3. Illinois
4. Washington
5. Michigan

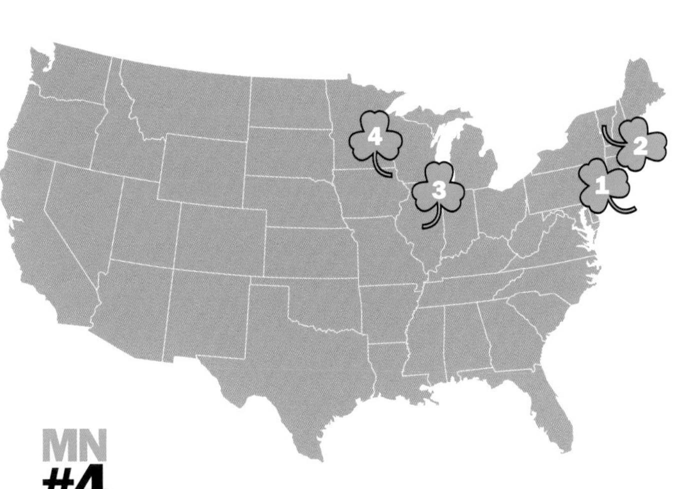

MN
#4

Cities with Most Irish Decendents:

1. New York
2. Boston
3. Chicago
4. **St. Paul**

Faeries

Troll

Sláinte

Skol

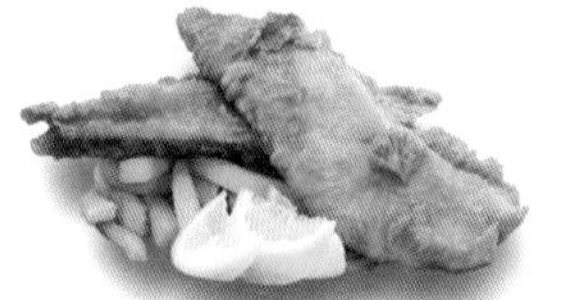

Fish & Chips

Lutefisk

Irish vs. Norwegian

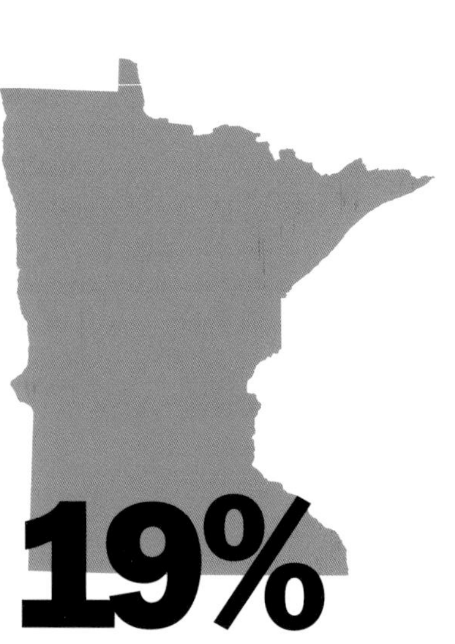

19%

Minnesota's population differs significantly from the rest of the U.S. with proportionally fewer people of Hispanic descent and a higher number of people from Asia and Africa. About 19% of Minnesotans are people of color.

After the Vietnam War, Minnesotans opened their hearts, homes, and wallets to welcome an exodus of Vietnamese, Laotian, Cambodian, and Hmong refugees. Currently, Minnesota is home to the second-largest concentration of Laotians in the nation.

MN
#1

This compassion continued in the 1990s with the largest influx of Somali and Ethiopian refugees in the nation. Recently, refugees from Myanmar (Burma), the Karen, chose St. Paul as their home. More than 8,000 Karen (the nation's largest population) currently live in St. Paul, and the city has the nation's first Karen police officer.

The nation's largest Somali, Tibetan, and Karen populations reside in Minnesota, as does the second-largest Hmong community. Minnesota is home to 13% of the nation's refugees.

Source: sturdevant/strib/ 2/5/17

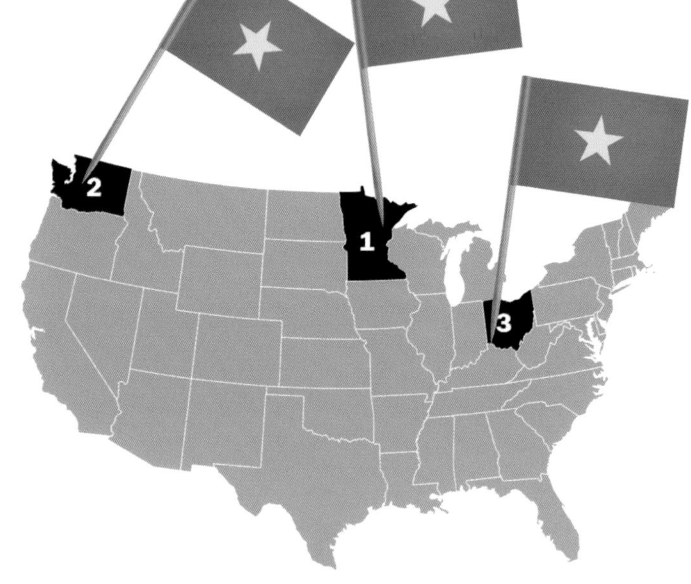

MN
#1

States with Most Somali Refugees:

1. Minnesota
2. Washington
3. Ohio

MN FACT

Minnesota has the highest per-capita adoptions from Korea.

Economic Disparities

This influx of immigrants, who frequently do not immediately find well-paying jobs or have stable incomes, tends to increase the serious economic disparities that exist between people of color and the white population in the state. According to the Pew Research Center, the wealth gap between white and black Minnesotans stands at its highest level since 1989. Minnesota ranks dead last with the highest median household income gap in the nation. High school graduation rates for African Americans in the Twin Cities have been disappointingly low, while 82% of Asian Indians in Minnesota have a bachelor's degree.

One Minnesotan in 14, or 6.9%, is foreign born. More than 300,000 Minnesotans speak English as a second language. Students enrolled in St. Paul public schools speak 125 different languages or dialects.

Only 1.3% of Minnesota's population is Native American. There are **7** Anishinaabe reservations and **4** Dakota communities in the state. 45% of Native Americans in the Twin Cities live in poverty. Little Earth, a 212-unit apartment complex with a wide array of social services in Minneapolis, is the nation's only public housing project that gives American Indians preference.

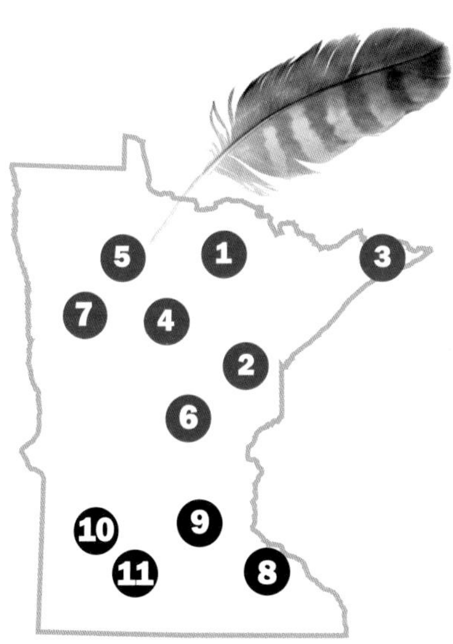

Minnesota Native American Communities:

1. Bois Forte
2. Fond du Lac
3. Grand Portage
4. Leech Lake
5. Red Lake
6. Mille Lacs
7. White Earth
8. Prairie Island
9. Shakopee Mdewakanton
10. Upper Sioux
11. Lower Sioux

Minnesota is home to 13,000 foreign students studying at Minnesota colleges and universities. Most of these students come from China, India, South Korea, and Taiwan.

"The University of Minnesota has the third-largest cohort of students on study abroad programs."

Eric Kaler
President, University of Minnesota

ARC
American Refugee Committee

The CENTER for VICTIMS of TORTURE
Restoring the Dignity of the Human Spirit

Given this history, it seems appropriate that Minnesota is the headquarters for two international organizations dedicated to serving refugees, the American Refugee Committee (ARC) and the Center for Victims of Torture (CVT). Last year, ARC assisted more than 3 million people in 11 different countries. CVT, founded in 1985 on the campus of the University of Minnesota, has provided healing, training, advocacy, and research to torture victims from 79 different countries. It currently operates programs in post-conflict communities in the Middle East and Africa.

top 10 Peace Corps

This cultural exchange goes in both directions. Minnesota ranks in the top 10 states in the nation for Peace Corps volunteers.

Islam

Christianity

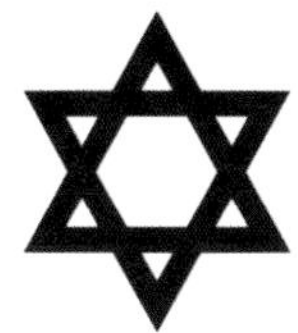

Judaism

Buddhism

Hinduism

agnosticism

Not Everyone is German or Swedish Lutheran

Christian: 74%
Mainline Protestant – 29%
Catholic – 22%
Evangelical Protestant – 19%
Mormon – 1%
Greek Orthodox, Jehovah's Witness, or other Christians – less than 3%

Non-Christian Faith: 4%
Jewish – 1%
Muslim – 1%
Buddhist and Hindu – less than 1%
Other world religions – 1%

Unaffiliated (Nonreligious): 20%
Agnostic – 4%
Atheist – 3%
Does not declare a religion – 13%

Don't know: 2%
ALSWT (Agnostical / Logistical Society of Wishful Thinkers) – One member, Gary Olin of Marine on St. Croix

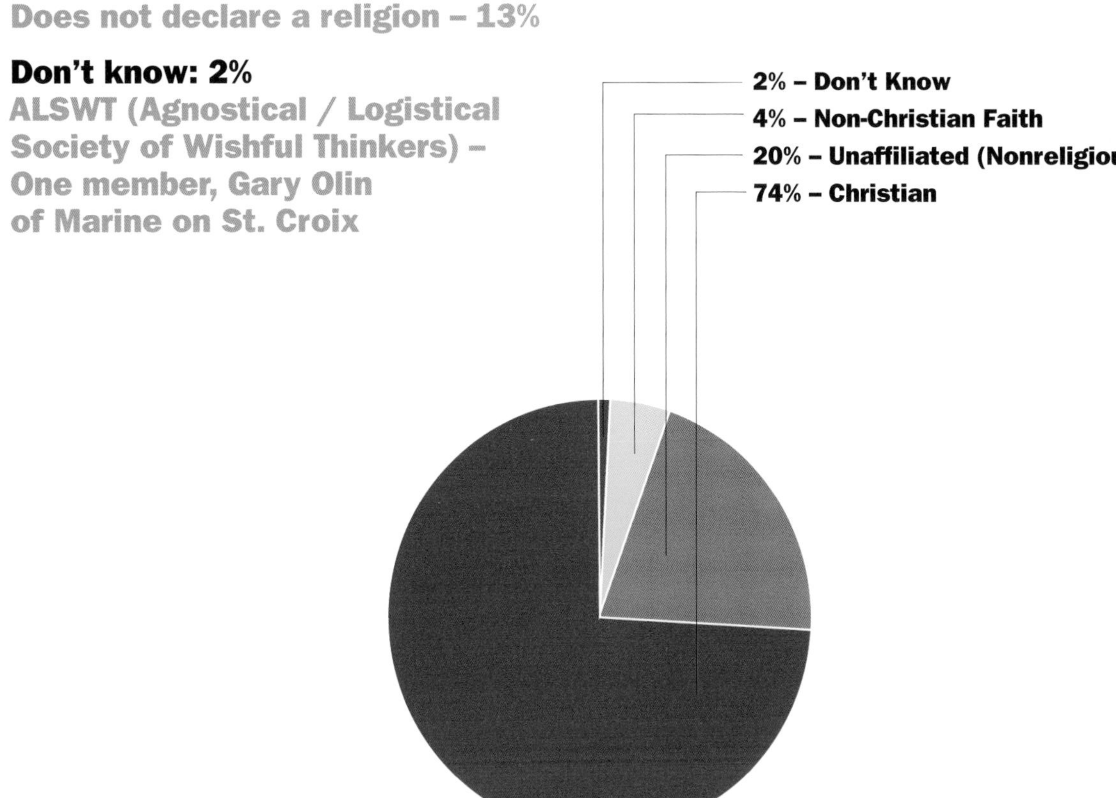

The largest Buddhist temple in the U.S. is in Minnesota. Pictured is the Watt Munisotaram, a Cambodian Buddhist temple near Hampton, MN.

Eagle Brook Church, Woodbury

Courtesy of BWBR Architects

Grace Church, Eden Prairie

Courtesy of Grace Cathedral

The LivingWord Christian Center, Brooklyn Park

© David Katzung/Courtesy of Living Word Christian Center

Wooddale Church, Eden Prairie

© Gallop Studios

Minnesota is also home to six megachurches. The largest is Eagle Brook, with six campuses (the largest in Woodbury) and more than 18,000 in attendance. (A megachurch is defined as having more than 2,000 members.)

Source: The Hartford Institute

MN FACT

The nation's largest Hindu Temple is in Maple Grove. There are 40,000 Hindus in Minnesota.

© Morgan Sheff Photography

Courtesy of the Office of Ilhan Omar

Ilhan Omar became the nation's first Somali American legislator when she was elected to the Minnesota House in 2016.

Abdi Warsame became the first Somali American on the Minneapolis City Council in 2013.

Courtesy of the Office of Abdi Warsame

Richard Tsong Taatarii,©2014, Star Tribune

In December of 2014, Ler Htoo became what is believed to be the first police officer from Myanmar's Karen ethnic group in the U.S.

Congressman Keith Ellison, who represents the Fifth District in Minneapolis, was the first Muslim elected to the U.S. House of Representatives.

David Joles, ©2006, Star Tribune

In 1933 Minnesota's progressive government prohibited discrimination based on sexual orientation and gender identity. **Minnesota was the first state in the nation to do so.** Same-sex marriage was legalized in 2013 in Minnesota.

Jeff Wheeler, ©2015, Star Tribune

The Twin Cities ranked sixth in LGBT-friendly cities and third in the nation in number of gay households. The World Professional Association for Transgender Health (WPATH) is located in Minneapolis.

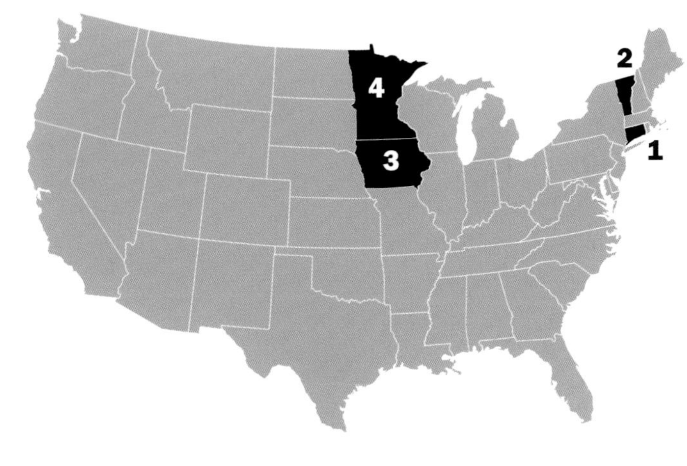

MN
#4

States with the Most Gay-Friendly Companies:

1. Connecticut
2. Vermont
3. Iowa
4. **Minnesota**

Minnesota is clearly a good place for women and children. Women are valued, as evidenced by their prominence in government and business. Minnesota is the best state in the nation for women based on working conditions, work–family balance, career opportunities, safety, and political participation.

Source: washingtonpost.com/blogs/govbeat

Chapter 10.
Women and children first.

Minnesota women were key players in the national fight for women's suffrage. In 1881, the Minnesota Woman Suffrage Association was founded in Hastings, MN. The MWSA hosted the American Woman Suffrage Association's annual conference in 1885, which brought the MWSA and women's suffrage in Minnesota to the national stage.

MN
#2

Women's Participation in Political Activities:

1. New Hampshire
2. **Minnesota**
3. Maine
4. Washington
5. Massachusetts

Source: statusofwomen.org/about-us

Marlene Johnson #42
1983–1991 DFL

Joanell Dyrstad #43
1991–1995 Independent Republican

Joanne Benson #44
1995–1999 Independent Republican

Mae Schunk #45
1999–2003 Reform/Independence

Carol Molnau #46
2003–2011 Republican

Yvonne Prettner Solon #47
2011–2015 DFL

Tina Smith #48
2015–present DFL

The Women Presidents' Organization (WPO) has blossomed in Minnesota in the past dozen years, with six chapters of 20 female CEOs each and a waiting list for the seventh chapter. The WPO has 125 chapters on six continents. **No other city in the country has more chapters than Minneapolis.**

Source: MNbusiness, *Jan 2016*

Minnesota is one of the only states to have formed a statewide Women's Consortium. It is comprised of approximately 150 organizations and works "to achieve equity and justice for women and their families."

Source: mnwomen.org/about-us

Minnesota has had the most female lieutenant governors in the nation, although the state has not elected a female governor yet. It has the fourth-highest number of women in the state house, and U.S. Senator Amy Klobuchar has represented the state for two terms. It also **ranks fifth in the nation for proportion of women in state legislatures.**

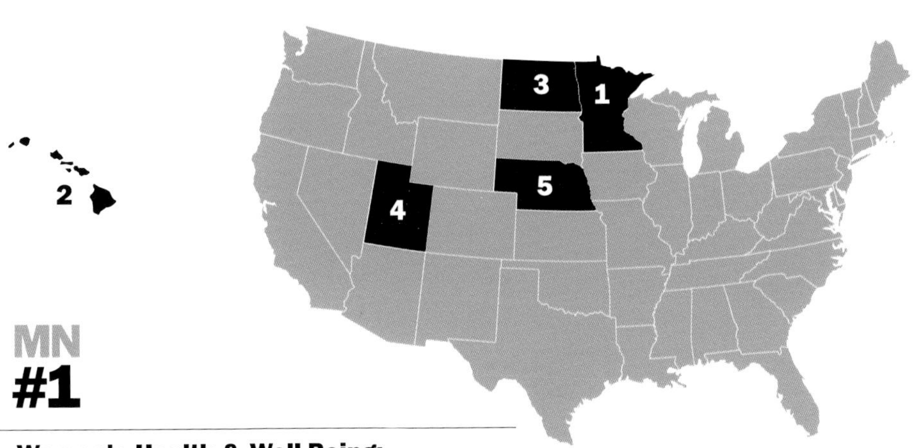

MN
#1

Women's Health & Well-Being:

1. **Minnesota**
2. Hawaii
3. North Dakota
4. Utah
5. Nebraska

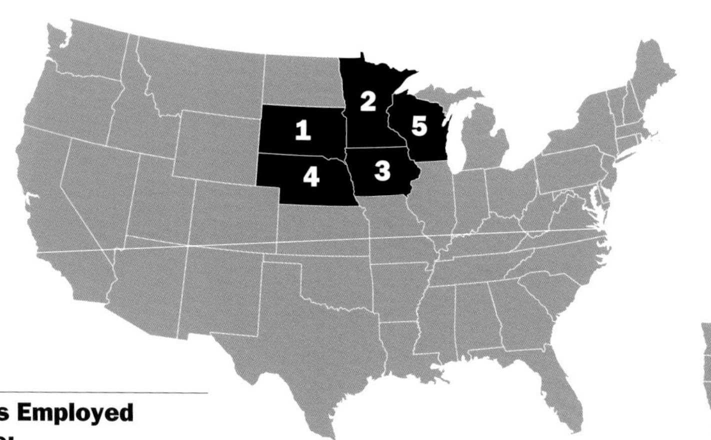

MN #2

Best for Mothers Employed Outside of Home:

1. South Dakota 84%
2. **Minnesota 81%**
3. Iowa 81%
4. Nebraska 81%
5. Wisconsin 80%

Source: startribune.com 5/5/16

Minnesota is second in the percentage of mothers who are employed outside the home. The Midwest has the hardest-working moms in the nation: South Dakota, Minnesota, Iowa, Nebraska, and Wisconsin.

Nationally, 73% of women with children under the age of 18 work outside the home, compared to 82% in Minnesota. It is 11th in top states for working moms when considering such factors as childcare costs, parental leave, and gender pay gap.

Source: ipums-usauofm

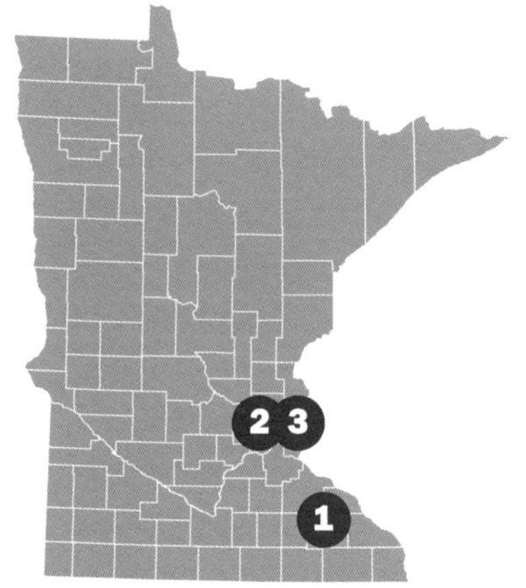

Best Cities for Women in Workforce:

1. Rochester
2. Minneapolis
3. St. Paul

Women's earnings, labor force participation rate, cost of living, and employment rate are among the criteria used in the study. nerdwallet.com 4/12/16

MN #1

Rochester is the best place in the country for working women, according to SmartAsset. The personal finance consultancy cited Rochester's narrow gender pay gap and steady employment for women.

Source: Minnesota Department of Employment and Economic Development Weekly Digest Bulletin

MN #1

Best Over-All State for Women:

1. **Minnesota**
2. Massachusetts
3. Vermont
4. Maryland
5. New Hampshire

Source: WalletHub 2015

Women's Foundation
Created in 1983, it was **the first women's foundation in the nation and is the largest today.** It applies a rigorous intersectional perspective to all its work—grant making, research, and public policy. It is dedicated to ensuring that gender, race, and equity (class, age, ability, LGBT, and immigrant status) are taken into consideration in all its work.

Womenwinning is a multipartisan fundraising and political training organization that promotes pro-choice women candidates for elective office. It has been instrumental in helping Minnesota achieve its ranking in the number of women in elective office.

Minnesota Women's Economic Roundtable (MWER)
The MWER has 130 members from the professions, small and large businesses, nonprofits, and government. Founded in 1979, it is a forum for women leaders to gather and discuss broad economic issues and their implications for local communities.

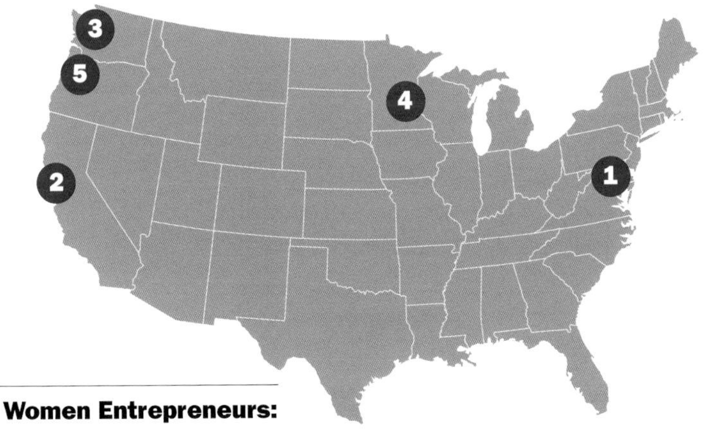

MN
#4

Top Cities for Women Entrepreneurs:

1. Washington, DC
2. San Francisco
3. Seattle
4. **Minneapolis**
5. Portland

© David Sherman

The Minnesota Lynx is a women's professional basketball team based in Minneapolis. The team was founded in 1999 and has won three WNBA Championships. Lynx players are viewed as significant role models for young girls in the state and have helped to increase the number of young women playing sports.

WNBA Champions:

2011

2013

2015

2016—nearly*

2017

*The league acknowledged the day after the final game that a timing error caused the Lynx to lose.

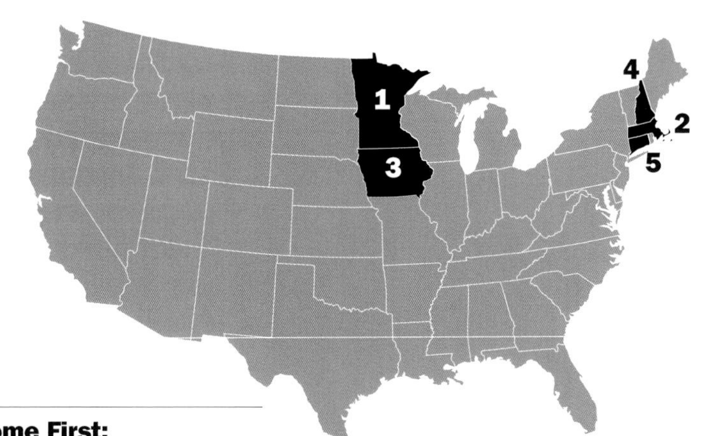

MN #1

Children Come First:

1. Minnesota
2. Massachusetts
3. Iowa
4. New Hampshire
5. Connecticut

Source: WalletHub 2015

MN ranks number one in the nation in overall child well being despite having significant racial disparities among its children.vt

Where Children Are #1

Minnesota ranks as the most kid-friendly state for the second year in a row, according to the Annie E. Casey Foundation's *Kids Count* report. The ranking uses a careful methodology to tally each state's composite score in four main categories: economic and health conditions, education, and quality of communities.

© iGrekov's/Shutterstock

Children's Defense Fund (CDF) Minnesota

The Children's Defense Fund–Minnesota, one of eight state affiliates of the national Children's Defense Fund, is dedicated to ending child poverty. It is part of a statewide coalition, Kids Can't Wait, that advocates for affordable and accessible childcare for Minnesota families.

Minnesota leads in combating child sex trafficking. The legislature passed and funded the Safe Harbor Law, which has decriminalized prostitution and provided 10 "navigators" to guide kids out of trafficking. Minnesota spends more than any other state on this issue.

Source: MPR *5/17/16*

Children of color make up 30% of children under five in the state. 14% are living in poverty vs. the national average of 22%. 29% of Minnesota's children live in a single-parent household. Minnesota ranks **second in best states for underpriviledged children,** based on factors including lowest percentages of mistreated children, food insecurity rate, and children in single-parent families.

© Dan Anderson

Nation's Tallest Water Slide
The water park near the Mall of America is 10 stories high and boasts the tallest water slide in the nation.

© Science Museum of Minnesota

The Science Museum
National Geographic Traveler named the Science Museum of St. Paul in the **top 10 in the nation.**

Circus Juventas
Based in St. Paul, Circus Juventas is the **largest children's circus training school in the U.S.,** with more than 1,000 students learning circus arts and activities.

© Bill Raab

STEPPINGSTONE THEATRE
FOR YOUTH DEVELOPMENT

St. Paul's Steppingstone Theatre
Another award-winning children's theater in Minnesota. Backstage.com ranks Steppingstone as one of the 12 great children's theaters in the nation.

MN #2

Largest Indoor Playground:

1. Orlando
2. **Edina**

Edinborough Park's Adventure Peak in Edina is the second-largest indoor playground in the nation. Orlando's Galaxy Fun is #1.

Courtesy of CTC

The Children's Theatre

The Tony Award–winning theater in Minneapolis is ranked #2 in the world by *Time* magazine based on number of tickets sold and number of productions. Moscow's children's theater is ranked #1. A recent musical production of *Diary of a Wimpy Kid: The Musical* is yet another one of its successes headed for Broadway.

Courtesy of St. Cloud Convention and Visitors Bureau

More than 90% of children in Minnesota participate in one or more activities outside of school (i.e., sports, lessons, and clubs) compared to 80% nationwide.

Source: childrens health data.org

The Three Zoos of MN

The Duluth Zoo and the Como Park Zoo in St. Paul offer close-up viewing of big cats, polar bears, and grizzlies. The Minnesota Zoo has a world-class collection of cold-climate animals. Its Russia's Grizzly Coast was fifth of the top 10 winners in the country for Best Zoo Exhibit.

The award-winning new Guthrie Theater opened in 2006.

Chapter 11.
The curtain is always going up.

Courtesy of Guthrie Theater

75 MN

According to the Ivey's, the nonprofit annual theater award show, there are currently 75 professional theaters in Minnesota, a large majority located in the Twin Cities. The Guthrie, as well as the other professional theaters, pays enough in salaries and stipends to support a large number of actors, technicians, and management personnel to attract talent from around the nation.

Courtesy of Stratford Festival

In 1963, when Sir Tyrone Guthrie selected Minneapolis over other competing cities to become the dominant regional repertory theater in the nation, the Twin Cities quickly became a "theater town." Rather than reduce the number of smaller theaters (200 to 600 seats) dozens more were formed, funded by corporations, foundations, and individuals.

"Shh, let's keep this to ourselves. As an actor in the Twin Cities, I live somewhere between pride and fear. Pride that our cities support a vibrant truly progressive theater scene. This is a community that encourages new work, companies large and small, challenging ideas, and innovative productions by financially enabling the work and, as importantly, actually seeing it. Fear that our theater scene will become 'known' to the rest of the country and we will be inundated with actors moving here to make the kind of careers they had always hoped to have."

Sally Wingert

(in Peg Guilfoyle's book Offstage Voices)

© Cameron Wittig

In the early 1980s, as new theaters were being built and old ones were renovated, trepidation grew in the theater community over the surge in Broadway touring productions coming to the Twin Cities.

The building of the new Ordway in St. Paul and the renovations of the majestic State and Orpheum Theatres in Minneapolis created more than 6,000 new seats to fill in over 24 weeks of big productions. Rather than raiding audiences from smaller venues, these new theaters created a whole new class of audience, lovers of American musical theater. Audience profiles did not significantly overlap as was feared. To the contrary, these new theaters may have enticed Broadway audiences to venture out to smaller venues.

How much theater is too much? It seems at times that there can't be too much. In February of 2015 there were seven opening nights in the Twin Cities on the same evening! A theater aficionado hardly has time to see everything. On any given night there may be 10 to 20 options for a committed viewer.

Courtesy of U of M Archives

In the 1950s, Dr. Frank Whiting of the University of Minnesota's theater department was instrumental in creating outstanding productions and training actors who went on to become the nucleus of the Twin Cities' new theater movement.

MN FACT

Minnesota and the Twin Cities were theatrical backwaters in the 1930s and 40s. A few traveling shows occasionally played the string of theaters on Hennepin Avenue in downtown Minneapolis. Minneapolis' only theatrical claim to fame at that time was that it was the #1 city in the nation for designing and fabricating theatrical backdrops for college and high school plays. St. Paul was #2 in the nation. That faux living room wall used in your high school acting debut most likely came from the Twin Cities.

© Dan Anderson

On a per-capita basis, the Twin Cities are second only to New York City in number of theater tickets sold.

In 2014 the Orpheum Theatre was fifth in the world for ticket sales. (The Target Center was 17th in ticket sales for music.)

Source: Pollstar

A Creative Vitality Index (CVI) report in 2013 ranked the Twin Cities fifth in the nation. The CVI measures the economic impact of creative industries on local communities. Jon Spayde, in *The Line* newsletter, reported that the Twin Cities' creative sector contributed $700 million to the local economy. That figure rose to $831 million in 2014. More than 20,000 people, in 5% of the jobs in the Twin Cities, are employed in the sector. The per-capita rate of **theater company revenue in the Twin Cities is 14 times the national average.**

MN #5

Creative Vitality Index (CVI):

1. Washington, DC
2. New York City
3. Los Angeles
4. Boston
5. **Twin Cities**

The Palace Theatre in downtown St. Paul reopened in December 2016 after being dormant for 40 years. The charming 2,800-seat venue will feature contemporary music.

3/8 of 1% tax

Helping Future Vitality

In 2013, during the height of the recession, Minnesotans agreed by a two-to-one majority to tax themselves to support the environment and the arts. This was the largest arts and cultural ballot initiative in American history. Minnesota is the only state in the union with dedicated funding for the arts in its state constitution. A sales tax of three-eighths of 1% generated over $58 million in 2015 and will continue to produce revenue for the arts for the remainder of the 25 years of the amendment.

The Playwrights' Center

Founded in 1971, the center focuses on supporting playwrights and promoting new and innovative plays to production at theaters across the country. Membership is open to all and provides nearly 2,000 playwrights worldwide with tools, resources, and support.

Source: info@pwcenter.org

The Twin Cities' robust theater community has a significant financial impact on the Twin Cities that most people don't think about.

The Lion Thing

The Twin Cities' large theatrical infrastructure and enthusiastic musical theater audiences enticed Disney to build and launch the world-famous show *The Lion King* at the Orpheum Theatre in 1998. Since that time the show has grossed over $6.2 billion and has been seen by more than 85 million people throughout the world.

440

Minnesota has 440 theaters, 200 outside the metropolitan area. Scores of community theaters across the state are enjoying continued success.

The Old Log Theatre on the shores of Lake Minnetonka in Excelsior is the oldest professional theater in Minnesota, and is often cited as **the oldest continuously operating professional theater in the U.S.**

The nonprofit Penumbra Theatre in St. Paul is the **nation's longest-running African American theater.** Two-time Pulitzer Prize winner August Wilson launched his career at the Penumbra.

Dudley Riggs's Brave New Workshop in downtown Minneapolis is **the oldest comedy satire theater in America.** Alums include Louie Anderson, Al Franken, and Penn and Teller.

© Emily Utne

THEATER
LATTÉ
DA
THEATER MUSICALLY

Founded in 1998 by Peter Rothstein and Denise Prosek, Theater Latté Da is in its 18th year. They have presented outstanding musicals like *Ragtime*, which enjoyed a sold-out run in 2016.

The Children's Theatre of Minneapolis is believed to be the #1 children's theater in the U.S., based on number of tickets sold and number of productions, and #2 in the world (Moscow's children's theater is #1).

The Chanhassen Dinner Theatre, founded in 1968, is the nation's largest professional dinner theater, with three Equity theaters under one roof.

MN
#1&3

Fringe Festival is **the nation's largest non-juried fringe festival** and third-largest juried (NYC and Orlando are 1st and 2nd). The Fringe features 850 performances in an 11-day period. Performances are awarded on a lottery basis and are attended by more than 50,000 people.

Some other well-known theaters in the Twin Cities include:

Park Square Theatre
Mixed Blood Theatre
The Jungle Theater
Steppingstone Theatre
History Theatre

Ten Thousand Things Theater brings high-quality theater to those with limited access to the arts. State prisons are frequent venues for the theater troupe.

MN
#1
biggest

Artspace is the nation's largest developer of low-cost living spaces for artists.

Northern Spark is an annual all-night event that in 2016 focused on the theme of climate change and featured video projections, concerts, installations, and performances at a number of sites across the Twin Cities.

© Steve Skjold /Alamy

Chapter 12.

Many, many museums.

With more than 600 museums, Minnesota has twice as many per capita as any other state.

Weisman Art Museum, located on the campus of the University of Minnesota, has been a teaching museum since 1934. It is now known as a modern art museum and has a collection of more than 20,000 images. The museum occupies an iconic building designed by Frank Gehry that has become a major landmark for not only the University but also the state of Minnesota.

MN #5

The Walker Art Center is internationally recognized as a leading contemporary arts venue. **It ranks fifth in attendance in the United States.** The reconstruction of the adjacent Minneapolis Sculpture Garden resulted in 19 acres of sculpture and design, including the iconic fountain sculpture *Spoonbridge and Cherry,* by Claes Oldenburg and Coosje van Bruggen. It is believed to be **America's largest urban sculpture garden.**

© Morgan Sheff Photography

© Wayne Moran

© Minneapolis Institute of Art

Mia

Mia, formerly the Minneapolis Institute of Art, houses more than 89,000 art objects from around the world, including one of the most extensive Asian art collections in the country. Mia is widely acknowledged as one of the top museums in the nation.

© Dreamstime

A 2016–17 blockbuster exhibition featured historical objects and artworks highlighting the complex relationship between Martin Luther and the Age of the Reformation. On loan from Germany, many for the first time, were a few of Luther's personal possessions and a piece of furniture from his home, as well as paintings, sculpture, priests' robes, and orbs from the period. Together these objects told the story not only of Martin Luther's life but also of a significant moment in world history.

Admission to the museum is free to all, thanks in part to a Hennepin County tax and generous corporate and philanthropic support.

© Studio 306

The Museum of Russian Art is the only one of its kind in North America, with **the largest collection of Russian art outside of Russia.** In addition to its collection, the museum hosts temporary exhibitions of art and artifacts and offers lectures, seminars, and special events.

Source: tmork.org

Isaak Levitan (1892) Public Domain

1|4 MN

Science Museum of Minnesota

National Geographic Traveler ranks St. Paul's Science Museum in the **top 10 in the nation**. The National Science Foundation has awarded the Science Museum of Minnesota $52.5 million for science education and research, one of the highest amounts ever awarded to a museum. It houses one of only four authentically reconstructed dinosaurs in the world.

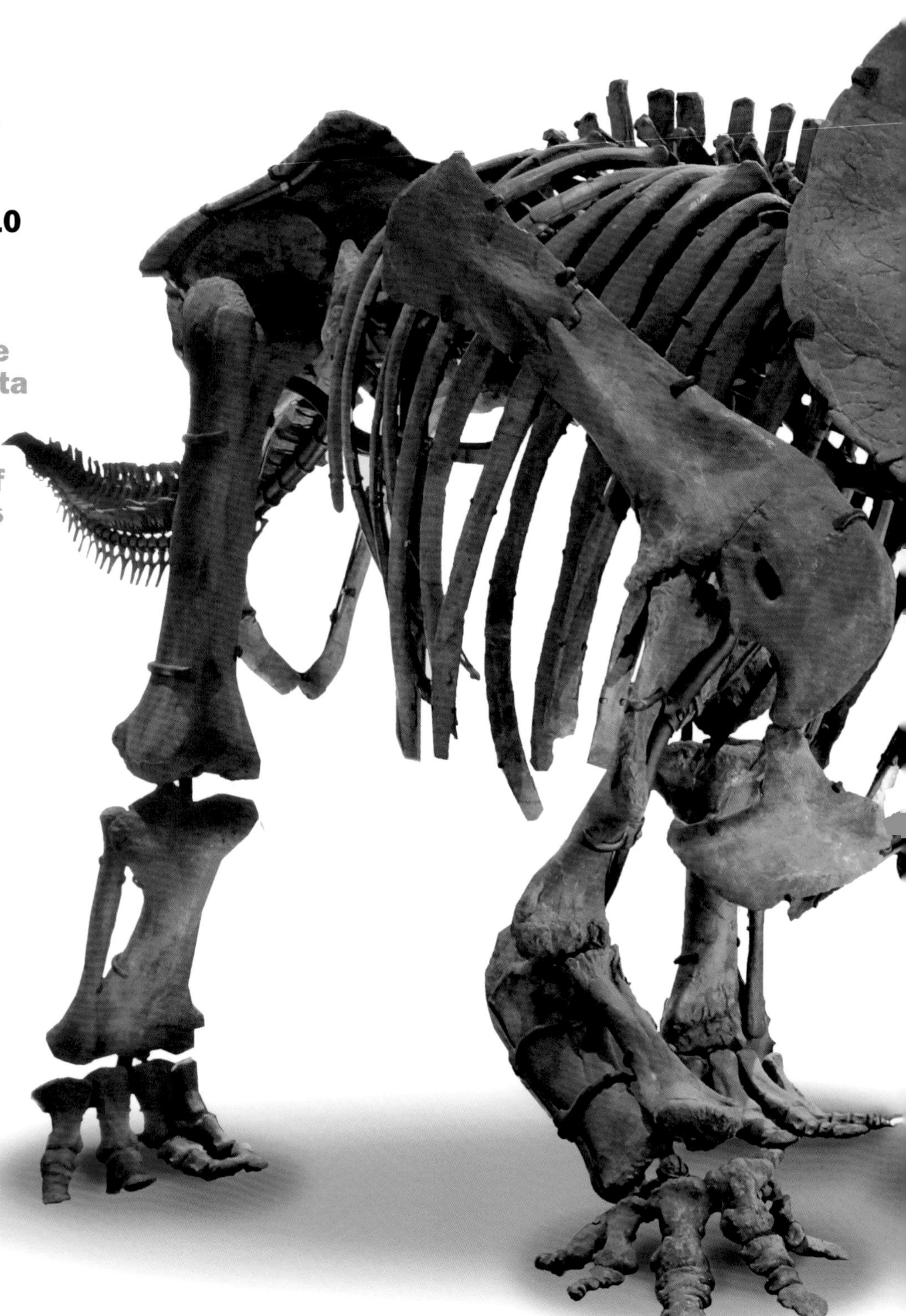

The Bakken Museum

Earl Bakken, the founder of Medtronic, created the museum to preserve the role and history of electricity and magnetism in life, and to explore the use of electricity in medicine. In addition to quirky displays and experiments, it hosts a casket in the basement that has been known to scare the wits out of kids (and adults). The library owns a first edition of Mary Shelley's 1818 classic, *Frankenstein*. In 2016 the Bakken launched a partnership with the Smithsonian Museum in Washington, DC.

Courtesy of Visit Saint Paul

SPAM Museum

Made of pig parts and secret spices, SPAM is the undisputed king of mystery meat. The meat is cooked in its own can right on the assembly line. Tastings and a tour by a "Spambassador" make this one of the most unusual and fun museums in America. Located in Austin, the Spam Museum is about 90 minutes south of the Twin Cities.

The Minnesota Children's Museum

Located in downtown St. Paul, with satellites in the Mall of America and Rochester, the Children's Museum has hosted more than six million children and their families, who "discovered the spark of learning through play." Newly renovated and expanded, the facility is continually updating its many interactive exhibits. Recently named **one of the 10 best children's museums in America.**

Source: grandparents.com

top **10** MN

Top Children's Museums:

- Boston Children's Museum
- Children's Museum of Indianapolis
- City Museum, St. Louis
- COSI, Columbus
- Exploratorium, San Francisco
- **Minnesota Children's Museum, St. Paul**
- Liberty Science Museum, Jersey City
- Please Touch Museum, Philadelphia
- Port Discovery Children's Museum, Baltimore
- The Strong National Museum of Play, Rochester, NY

© Brandon Stengel, farmkidstudios.com

Minnesota History Center

Home to the Minnesota Historical Society's vast collections, the History Center's museum and library provide a place for visitors to discover their links and connections to the past. The center, built in 1992, has been called by some the finest building constructed in Minnesota since the state capitol was completed in 1905.

The History Center houses, among many other things, 4,000 Minnesota newspapers and magazines, 1.2 million archaeological objects, and 174,000 books in 427,000 square feet.

Mill City Museum

Built into the ruins of what was once the world's largest flour mill, Mill City Museum is located on the historic Mississippi River. True-to-scale graphics of milling machines are featured on an eight-story glass façade, giving visitors an idea of how massive and significant the milling operation was in its heyday. A daily simulation of an explosion caused by flour dust stresses the hazards that once were rampant in mills and surprises even the most jaded or prepared audience.

The Bell Museum of Natural History and Planetarium

Located on the campus of the University of Minnesota, the Bell Museum explores the origins of the universe through the flowering of life on Earth to the formation of Minnesota's diverse habitats. Gallery exhibits tell a global story from a uniquely Minnesotan perspective with realistic dioramas and a state-of-the-art public planetarium.

©Paul Carroll

© Andre Jenny/Alamy

Lake Superior Marine Museum

Located in Duluth's Canal Park, this museum exhibits the history and operations of the Upper Great Lakes and Duluth's Aerial Lift Bridge.

Hjemkomst Center

The 76-foot replica of a Viking funeral ship was built by Robert Asp of Moorhead, MN, and sailed 6,000 miles from Duluth to Oslo, Norway, in 1982. The boat resides at the Hjemkomst Center in Moorhead.

© Greg Asp, courtesy of the Historical and Cultural Society of Clay County

© Davin Wait, courtesy of the Historical and Cultural Society of Clay County

When you think of the music scene in the Twin Cities, your thoughts go to the giants: Prince and Dylan. They began a legacy of placing the Twin Cities in the top 10 in the nation's music scene for many years. Livability.com's most recent ranking placed the Twin Cities in the top tier of music cities along with New York City, Los Angeles, Nashville, and New Orleans.

© Steven Cohen

Chapter 13.
Prince & Dylan. That about says it all.

Ravel's *Gaspard de la Nuit* appears on a prominent wall mural in downtown Minneapolis.

© Dan Anderson

Minnesota Music Notables

Prince
Bob Dylan
The Replacements
Soul Asylum
Semisonic
Babes in Toyland
The Andrews Sisters
Hüsker Dü
Paul Westerberg
Steve McClellan*
Lizzo
Trampled by Turtles
Information Society
Cloud Cult
Mint Condition
Trip Shakespeare
The Trashmen
Sounds of Blackness
The Bad Plus
The Jets
Fred Krohn*
Mark Mallman
The Wallets
Beat the Clock

**Promoters*

The Suburbs
The Jayhawks
Har Mar Superstar
The New Standards
Doomtree
Low
Flamin' Oh's
Morris Day and the Time
Atmosphere
Happy Apple
Poliça
Jimmy Jenson
Tapes 'n Tapes
Eyedea
Charlie Parr
Heiruspecs
Alexander O'Neal
Michael Bland
Bash & Pop
Jimmy Jam and Terry Lewis
Koerner, Ray & Glover
Willie Murphy
Lipps Inc.
Lamont Cranston
Cornbread Harris
Jeremy Messersmith
The Steeles
Ipso Facto

"If you love music, Minnesota is a wonderful place to live. If you prefer your jazz cool, your gospel hot, your carols in Latin, your Tristan *in German, your Bach on bagels, your Broadway under the stars, your Baroque on sackbut, or your rock in Purple Rain, you will find it in ample quantities in Minnesota.*

Music was woven into the cultural fabric of Minnesota even before it became a state. Wave after wave of pioneers and immigrants brought musical traditions that became absorbed into our patterns of worship, entertainment, and celebration, and eventually into our basic expectations for enjoying lives well lived."

Dr. Sam Grabarski

Former executive director, Minnesota State Arts Board, former president of the Minneapolis Downtown Council, recovering concert bassoonist

George Byron Griffith

Prince, with his Paisley Park studio, became the most influential artist of his generation and the best live performer of his time.

Bob Dylan, who had five #1 albums on the Billboard 200 from 1974 to 2009, was born and raised in Minnesota and has continued on and off to maintain a home here. In 2016 Dylan received the Nobel Prize for Literature.

Minnesota Loves Its Music Festivals

In the summer alone, there are the Moondance Jammin Country Fest in Walker; Soundset festival of hip-hop in St. Paul (over 30,000 attended in 2015, making it the largest in the nation); Festival Palomino in Shakopee; the Basilica Block Party and Rock the Garden in downtown Minneapolis; WE Fest in Detroit Lakes, and numerous others.

Another star may soon rise out of the 89 Twin Cities bars and restaurants that have live music performances each week.

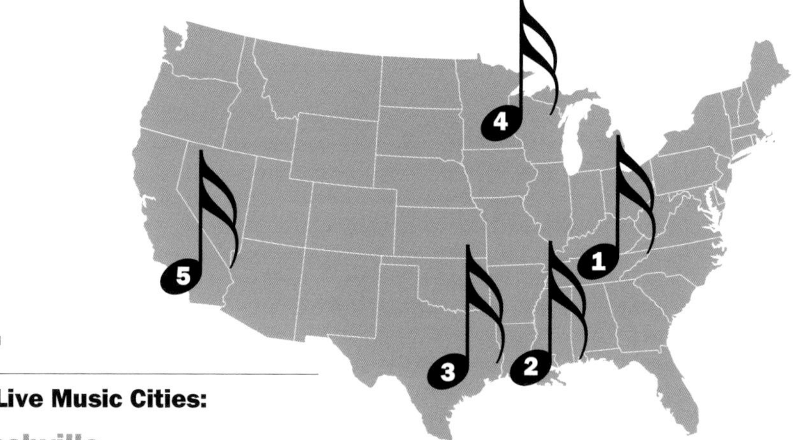

MN
#4

Best Live Music Cities:

1. Nashville
2. New Orleans
3. Austin
4. **Twin Cities**
5. Los Angeles

Source: livability.com

The largest free urban rock concert in Minnesota was in July of 1998, when Smashing Pumpkins played at the annual Hennepin Avenue Block Party in downtown Minneapolis as part of the Aquatennial Festival. 150,000 rocking fans covered Hennepin Avenue for blocks.

WE Fest Detroit Lakes

Festival Palomino Shakopee

© Darin Kamnetz

Rock the Garden Minneapolis

Soundset St. Paul

© Darin Kamnetz

© Darin Kamnetz

Basilica Block Party Minneapolis

Moondance Jammin Country Fest Walker

© Doug Heimstead

© Steve Loftness

© Darin Kamnetz

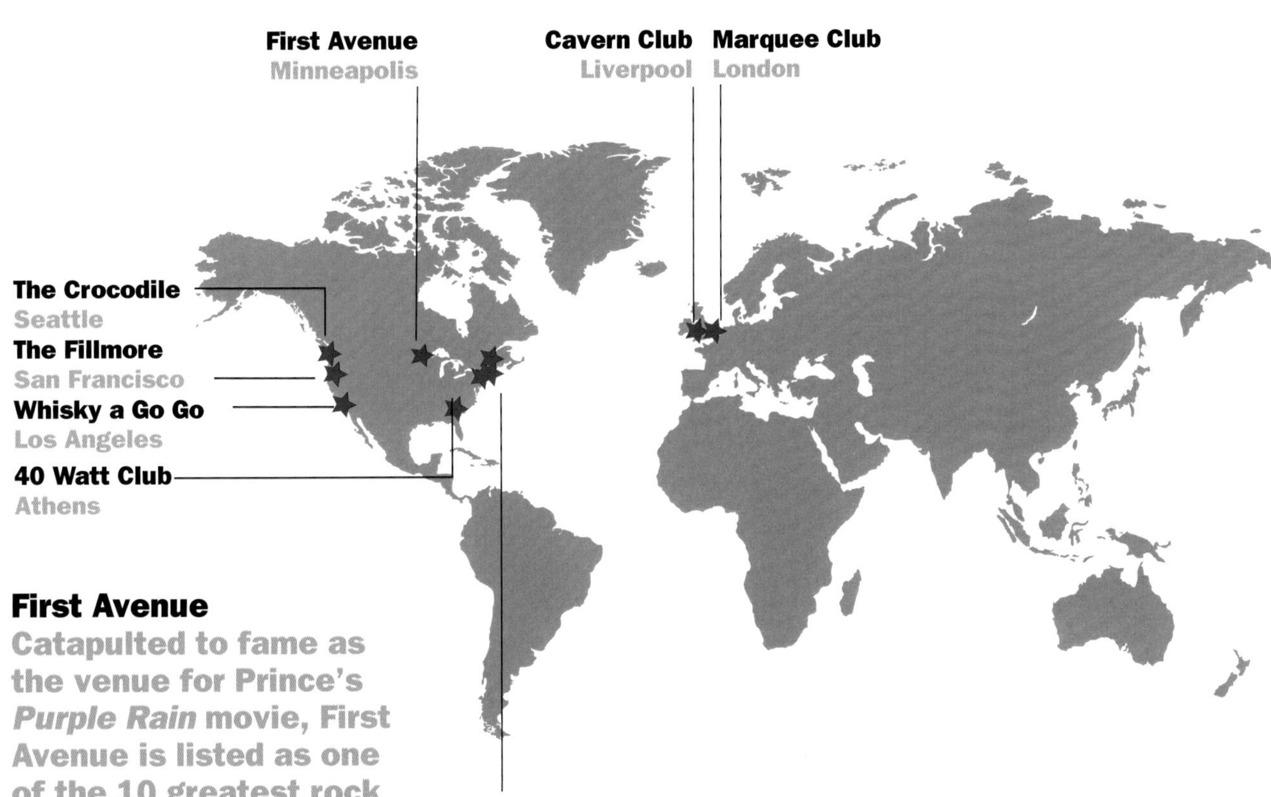

First Avenue

Catapulted to fame as the venue for Prince's *Purple Rain* movie, First Avenue is listed as one of the 10 greatest rock venues of all time, along with the Apollo in New York, Cavern Club in Liverpool, Whisky a Go Go in Los Angeles, and the Marquee Club in London. Top national and regional acts still perform there most nights of the year.

The Twin Cities have more than 3,500 live jazz performances each year, a feat on a per-capita basis that only New York City or New Orleans might equal.

The Dakota Jazz Club

Wynton Marsalis called the Dakota, owned and operated by impresario Lowell Pickett, one of the top five jazz clubs in the nation.

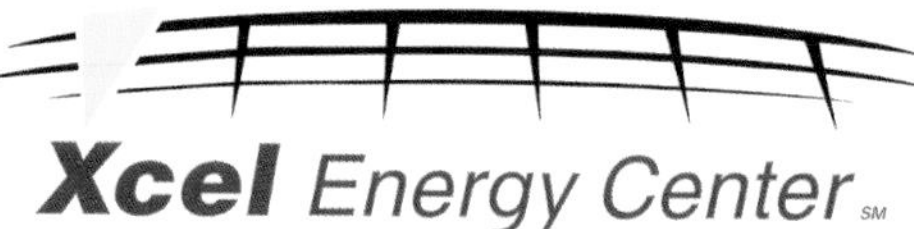

The Xcel Energy Center
St. Paul

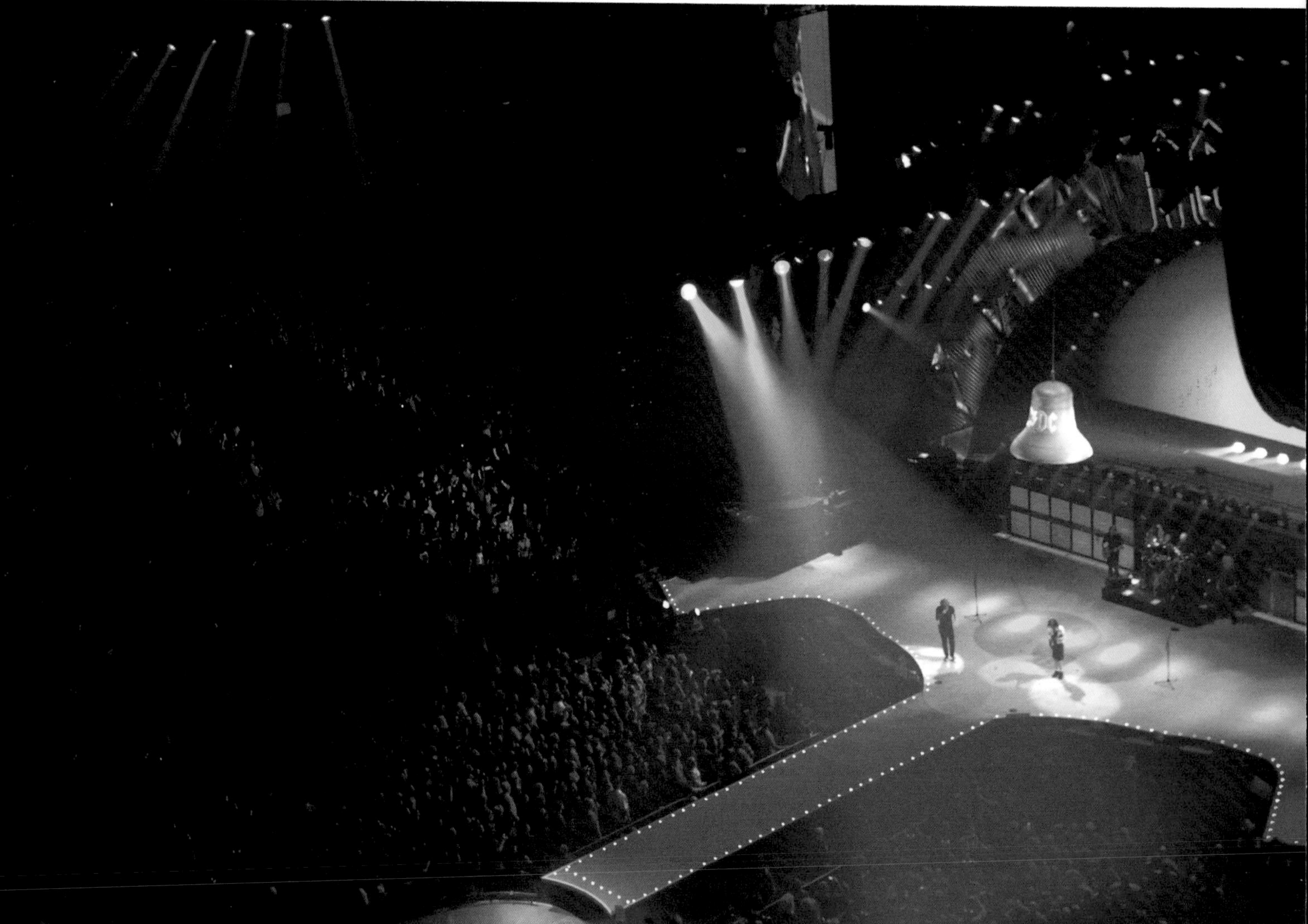

© Theodore Silviu/Alamy

© Bobak Ha'Eri

© AECOM

TARGET CENTER

The Target Center Minneapolis

Top performers sell more than 500,000 tickets each year between these two venues.

© Peter J. Sieger

Free Concerts by the Lake

The Lake Harriet Band Shell hosts free concerts throughout the summer. Patrons can hear a variety of music performed while watching sailboaters, paddleboarders, and kayakers enjoying the lake.

© Steven Cohen

Music at the Zoo

The outdoor amphitheater at the Minnesota Zoo in Apple Valley is an incredible summer music venue.

Garrison Keillor's *A Prairie Home Companion*, carried by more than 672 stations, is considered the most influential broadcast resource for folk music.

The St. Paul Chamber Orchestra is the nation's only full-time professional chamber orchestra and the finest such entity in the world.

© Greg Helgeson

The Minnesota Orchestra was founded as the Minnesota Symphony in 1902, the eighth orchestra in the nation to organize and perform. In the 1930s, under the direction of Eugene Ormandy, it became the most famous and recorded orchestra in the U.S. Now under the direction of Osmo Vänskä, it has been dubbed by a flock of New York music critics "the greatest orchestra in the world." In 2015 they were the first major orchestra to tour Cuba in over 50 years.

MN FACT

Professional orchestral managers contend that only six cities in the world have two internationally ranked orchestras, the Twin Cities among them. (International ranking requires regular touring and recording.)

The Greater Twin Cities Youth Symphonies is one of the largest youth orchestra programs in the nation, with year-round orchestras serving nearly 1,000 young musicians.

Also based in the Twin Cities, the Minnesota Youth Symphonies is devoted to developing young people's musical abilities through a conservatory approach.

The Bach Society of Minnesota The Bach Society is dedicated to performing the work of J. S. Bach. The Frederic Chopin Society and more than 90 other professional and civic ensembles perform throughout the year.

American Composers Forum The ACF is the nation's largest composer service organization in the country. Created to promote new contemporary classical music, the center links composers with performers to perfect their output. In 2006 the ACF launched the First Nations Composer Initiative to promote new music by Native American composers.

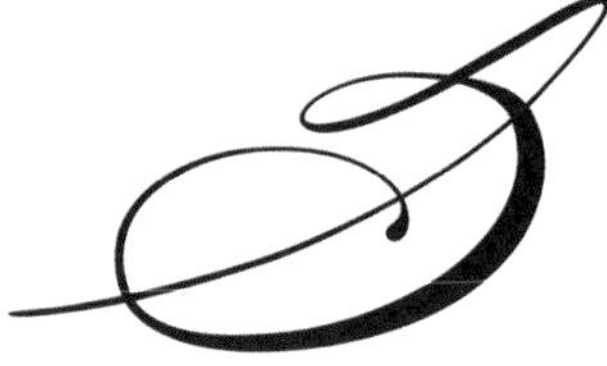

The Schubert Club Founded in 1882, the Schubert Club is unique in America for its concert series, scholarship competitions, recordings, and commissions of new music. Such musical luminaries as Yo-Yo Ma, Renée Fleming, Beverly Sills, and many more have established the club's prominent and distinguished reputation among the nation's musical organizations. The Schubert Club also houses the Schubert Museum, a world-class collection of historic keyboards and instruments from around the world.

MN #1

The Cedar Cultural Center has been named the best venue for world music, beating out St Ethelburga's in London, Ashkenaz in Berkeley, and Barbès in Brooklyn. World music is a category that encompasses different styles of music from around the globe.

MN FACT

Minnesota has the only remaining state band in the country. They have been playing great music for the past 120 years.

B sharp

B flat

A–© St Olaf Choir
B–© Bruce Silcox
C–Courtesy of David Hurst, Artistic Director
D–© Karl Demer
E–Courtesy of Minnesota Orchestra
F –© Paul Nixdorf & TC Gay Men's Chorus
G–© Terry Gydesen
H–© Heidi Garrido
I–Courtesy of Cantus

Choral Country
Most likely due to a strong Scandinavian influence, Minnesota's tradition of choral singing is so strong that the state has more choirs on a per-capita basis than any other state. *The New York Times International Datebook* calls the annual Christmas Festival of the **St. Olaf College Choirs (A)** "one of the five significant global holiday events."

VocalEssence (B)
Founded in 1969 by Philip Brunelle, the amazingly popular choir treats its audiences to seldom-performed choral works throughout the year. Its holiday program and multi-cultural WITNESS and ¡Cantaré! series are especially popular and serve as a basis for its educational outreach program. VocalEssense has commissioned more than 130 new works, ranging from small a cappella pieces to symphonic works.

Twin Cities Community Gospel Choir (C)
The nation's most gifted gospel singer, Robert "Eddie" Robinson, called by critics "the Pavarotti of Gospel," lives in Minnesota. Robinson leads the most decorated community-based gospel group, the Twin Cities Community Gospel Choir.

Sounds of Blackness (D)
Minnesota's gospel giant may be the only gospel choir in history to perform live in front of three broadcast audiences of one billion people each: the 1994 World Cup, 1996 Summer Olympics, and 1998 World Figure Skating Championships.

The Minnesota Chorale (E) The state's outstanding 150-voice symphonic chorus and 18 other choral organizations keep Minnesotans singing throughout the year.

The Twin Cities had the first gay and lesbian choirs in the nation.

Twin Cities Gay Men's Chorus (F)
Established in 1981, it today has a roster of 125 singers.

One Voice Mixed Chorus (G) 80 singers from the LGBT community.

Calliope Women's Chorus (H)
Dedicated to music by, for, and about women and social justice advocates for the lesbian community.

Cantus (I)
Acclaimed as "the premier men's vocal ensemble in the U.S.," according to *Fanfare*. Cantus engages audiences in a meaningful music experience and ensures the future of ensemble singing by mentoring young singers and educators. Cantus is a full-time ensemble of eight to 10 singers and has toured internationally.

© Stephen Maturen

Philip Brunelle conducting VocalEssence while on a European tour.

Courtesy of Ordway Theater

© Nic Lehoux

Concert Halls of Note Minnesota's performance venues rival the nation's finest. The acoustics in Orchestra Hall, renovated in 2015 and seating 2,077, and the Ordway Concert Hall, built in 2014 and seating 1,100, draw raves from audiences and

Courtesy of Cowles Center

© Morgan Sheff Photography

touring ensembles. Other halls of note are the Ordway Music Theater, St. Paul, built in 1985 and seating 1,900; the Cowles Center for Dance and the Performing Arts, refurbished in 2011 and seating 500; and Northrop Auditorium, renovated in 2014 and seating over 2,700.

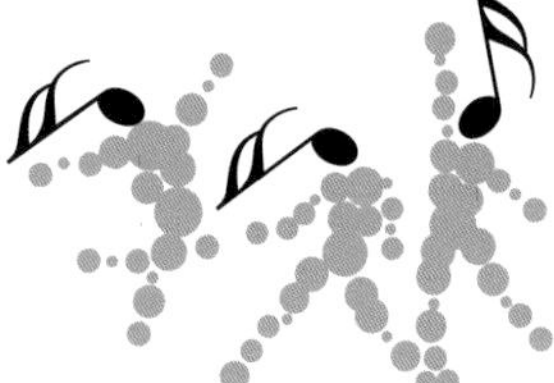

Hot Spot for Dance

The Twin Cities are home to one of the most thriving dance communities in the country. Of the local dance companies, 15 have annual budgets of over $1 million, and dozens of smaller companies showcase the work of hundreds of freelance dancers and choreographers. The Twin Cities are “a hot spot for dance” says Amy Fitterer, executive director of Dance/USA, a national service organization for American dance.

Minnesota Opera, First for World Premieres

Founded in 1963 and one of the nation’s largest and most distinguished professional opera companies, the Minnesota Opera boasts of having premiered the most new operas in the past 50 years. Its 2016 production of *The Shining* received rave reviews everywhere.

The MacPhail Center for Music

MacPhail is the oldest (1907) and largest music education nonprofit in the nation. Founded by a member of the Minneapolis Symphony Orchestra, William S. MacPhail, the school currently has 200 faculty members and serves 14,500 students learning 35 different instruments. Lawrence Welk was a graduate of MacPhail in 1927.

© MN Opera

THE COWLES CENTER
FOR DANCE & THE PERFORMING ARTS

The nation's dance community has focused on the Cowles Center for Dance and the Performing Arts in downtown Minneapolis. Besides New York City's Joyce Theater, there is no comparable facility in the nation. Housed in two buildings that were once two blocks apart, The Cowles Center is a catalyst for the creation, presentation, and education of dance. Its 500-seat theater hosts 20 leading dance and performing arts companies, including the well-known James Sewell Ballet and Zenon Dance Company.

The theater in the Cowles Center was designed specifically for dance, with a sprung floor, pit room for 40 musicians, large wing spaces, and a steep seating rake to give patrons an up-close view of the dancers.

© William Klotz

Record Move
In 1999 the Historic Shubert Theatre was incorporated into the Cowles Center. Weighing 5.8 million pounds, the building was moved two blocks over a 12-day period. It has the honor of being recognized by the *Guinness Book of Records* as the heaviest building ever moved on rubber tires.

© Scott Pakudaitis

Young Dance is a modern dance artistic and inclusive community focused on young people ages one to 18. Founded in 1987, it is dedicated to building both body and spirit through movement. Young Dance is one of many dance organizations that rehearse at the Cowles Center.

The University of Minnesota has a lively Theatre Arts and Dance Program.

© Brenda Carson / Shutterstock

Minnesota Dance Theatre and School

With a history spanning over half a century, the Minnesota Dance Theatre and School is an acclaimed arts leader in Minnesota. MDT is a place where professionals and students work together to share in the goals and accomplishments of dance.

Chapter 14. Just try to get bored.

Red Bull Crashed Ice competition.

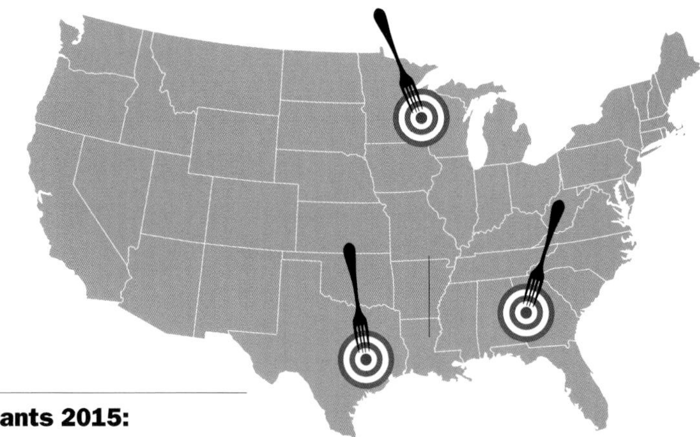

Food and Wine Magazine, in its July 2016 issue, placed Surly Brewing's upscale restaurant in the top 10 new restaurants in the U.S. Brewer's Table served four-course dinners with a flight of special beers designed for each course. In addition, Surly's informal beer hall holds 600 inside and hundreds more outside.

Most New Restaurants 2015:

1. Minneapolis
2. Austin
3. Atlanta

Source: CBS, January 2016

Dining Out

Minneapolis, Austin, and Atlanta had the most new restaurants opened in the nation in 2015. 100 were opened in Minneapolis alone.

Chef Jorge Guzman

The Bachelor Farmer and Spoon and Stable restaurants also garnered recent national acclaim for the Twin Cities.

Try hopping the 89 bars and restaurants with live music in the Twin Cities. There are hundreds more without live music. Visit one of the 100 craft brew pubs (40 were opened in the past three years).

100
Craft Brew Pubs

The North Shore Craft Beer Trail

The city's mayor has proclaimed Duluth the beer capital of Minnesota. Thousands of people attend the Summer Brew Fest each July to sample local artisanal brews.

MN
#4

Top Cities for Festivals:

1. New Orleans
2. Austin
3. Nashville
4. **Twin Cities**
5. Louisville

Source: travelleisure.com

Minnesota is in the top five nationally for festivals. Minnesota is also #1 per capita in fireworks shows. The Minneapolis Fourth of July fireworks display is one of the largest in the country.

Source: American Pyrotechnics Association

MN #1

MN State Fair Consistently Voted the Best:

1. **Minnesota**
2. Iowa
3. Massachusetts
4. Texas
5. Greater NY State Fair

The Minnesota State Fair is the nation's largest state fair based on average daily attendance, drawing 1.7 million visitors in a 12-day period. The Minnesota State Fair is second in overall attendance. The Texas State Fair draws an average of three million visitors, but over a 30-day period. Ohio is #3 in attendance, New York #4, and Iowa #5.

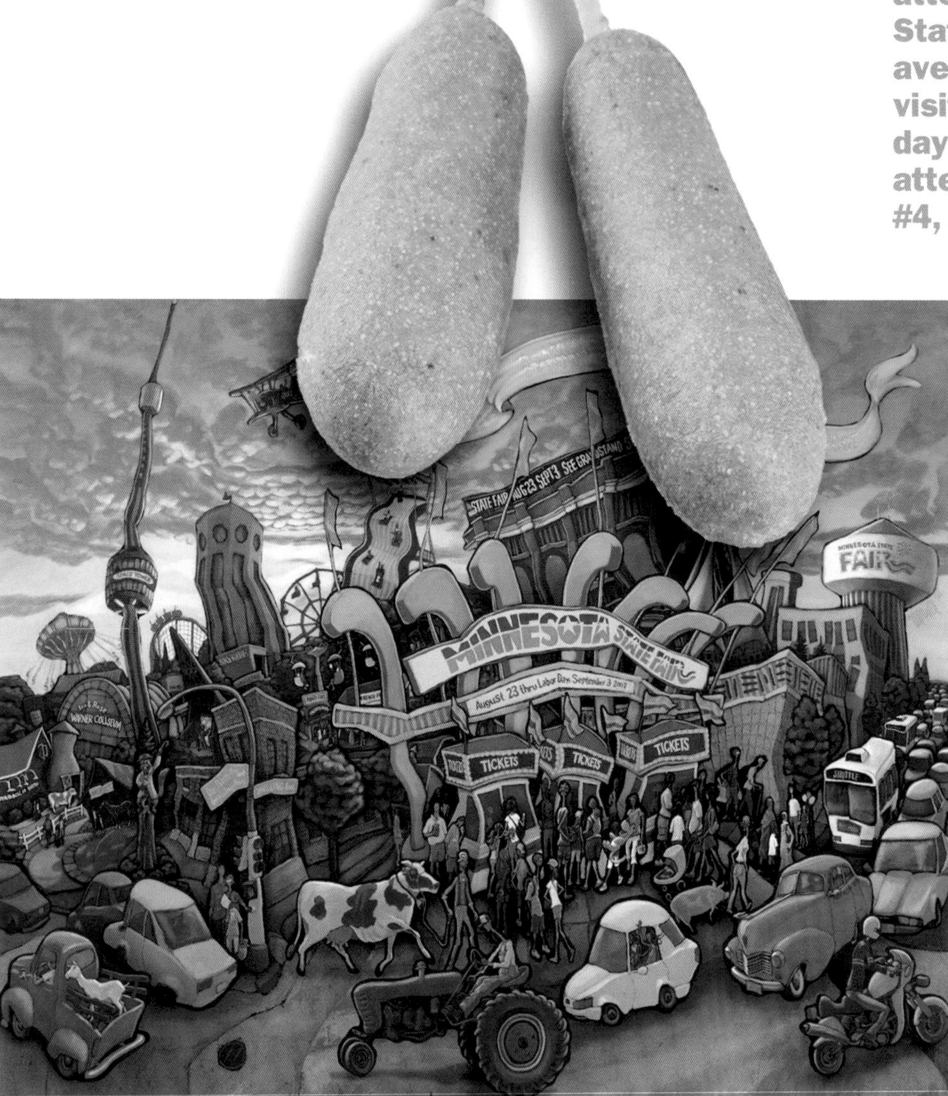

Courtesy of the Shakopee Mdewakanton Sioux Community

Mystic LAKE
CASINO • HOTEL

Mystic Lake Casino

The 460 members of the Shakopee Mdewakanton Sioux Community own and operate the Mystic Lake and Little Six casinos, making them the nation's richest tribe. The *New York Times* recently estimated that each member receives about $1 million a year.

As one of the largest Native American casinos in the U.S., Mystic Lake is located near the Twin Cities. The casino operates a 600-room hotel, five restaurants, a 2,100-seat auditorium, an 18-hole golf course, an 8,300-seat amphitheater and a convention center.

MN
#1

Apparently, Minnesotans love to gamble

In 2016 Minnesota was #1 in the nation for charitable gambling (pull tabs) at $1.5 billion. Washington is #2 at $800,000.

© Mega Pixel/Shutterstock

© Jeffery J Coleman / Dreamstime.com

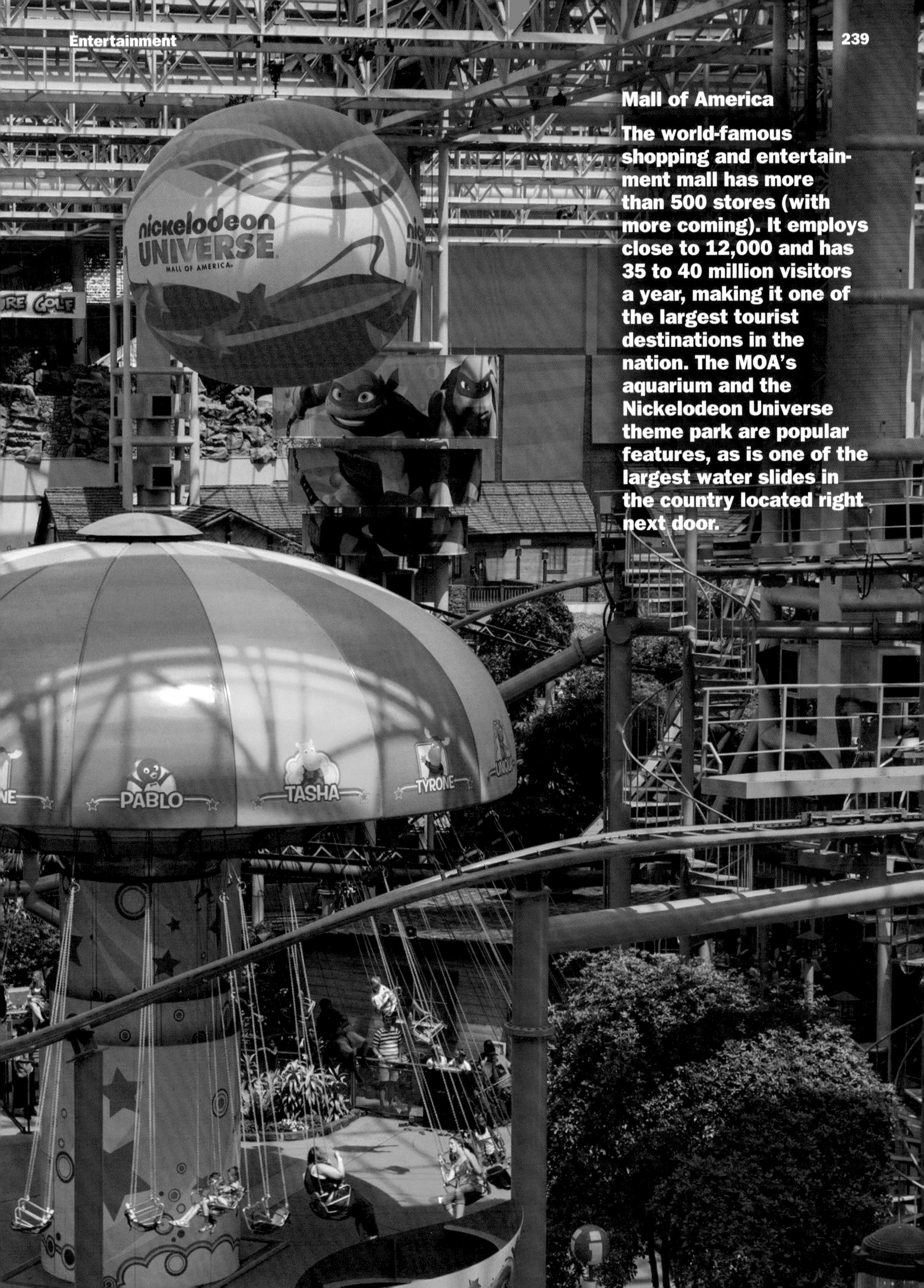

Mall of America

The world-famous shopping and entertainment mall has more than 500 stores (with more coming). It employs close to 12,000 and has 35 to 40 million visitors a year, making it one of the largest tourist destinations in the nation. The MOA's aquarium and the Nickelodeon Universe theme park are popular features, as is one of the largest water slides in the country located right next door.

The Dakota Jazz Club
Wynton Marsalis believes the Dakota is one of the top five jazz clubs in the country. The Dakota is open seven nights a week, showcasing performers from around the world.

WE Fest, a country western extravaganza, draws 90,000 each year to Detroit Lakes. It's the nation's largest camping and country music festival.

© Funniefarm5

© Johannes Cornelius/Shutterstock

Rock the Garden
at the Walker Art Center features 10 bands of national renown over two days and draws up to 12,000 enthusiasts. The Basilica Block Party, held just a few weeks later and less than a mile away, also draws thousands to listen to 25 bands on three stages.

First Avenue
is listed as one of the top 10 rock venues in America. The club was used for the filming of Prince's *Purple Rain.*

© Deonna Turner/Dreamstime

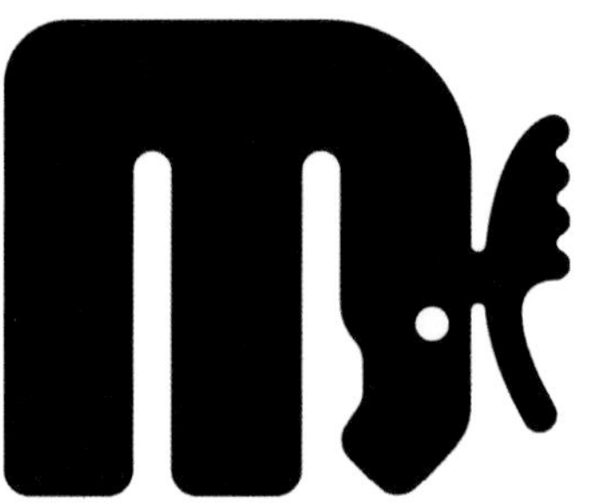

The Minnesota Zoo
not only houses the largest collection of animals from northern climes from around the world but also hosts concerts in its amphitheater, drawing thousands each summer.

Valleyfair, a 125-acre, 75-ride attraction, is a must-see for families. With eight rollercoasters, stage shows, and the Soak City water park, it'll take more than a day to fully experience. It's the largest amusement park in the Midwest.

© Panita Saripongse

The St. Paul Winter Carnival is 10 days of winter fun, ice sculptures, races, music, and parades. It is the nation's largest winter festival.

Free Concerts at the Lake Harriet Band Shell Experience music, ice cream, and lovely sailboats moored on the lake as people listen to nightly concerts throughout the summer.

Hazeltine National Golf Club hosts many premier golf tournaments. The prestigious Ryder Cup was held at Hazeltine in August 2016.

© ostill/123RF

2015

AQUATENNIAL

The Minneapolis Aquatennial is an annual celebration of summer, lakes, games, competitions, and parades. The 10-day event ends with the state's largest and most spectacular fireworks display.

The Renaissance Festival Started in Minnesota 46 years ago, the festival has the largest attendance in the U.S. Running from August through early October, the festival highlights fencing, jousting, comedy, shops, and medieval food and drink.

© nejron/123RF

© AECOM

MN FACT

Almost 500,000 entertainment tickets are sold annually between the Target Center in Minneapolis and the Xcel Center in St. Paul. The Target Center is the world's 17th-largest concert and special event venue.

Source: Pollstar 2014

ROALD AMUNDSEN

A grand celebration takes place in the Duluth Harbor each year when the tall ships arrive.

Major League Entertainment Options

Sports-crazy Minnesotans buy approximately six million professional and university sports tickets each year. Attendance figures bear this out:

At $50 for an average ticket (this is on the conservative side), **these teams generate more than $300 million in ticket sales.**

Vikings
419,440
tickets

Twins
2,200,000
tickets

Wild
779,774
tickets

Lynx
158,000
tickets

Timberwolves
600,000
tickets

Minnesota United
400,000
tickets (projected)

University of Minnesota
900,000
tickets (all sports)

Canterbury Downs
546,000
tickets

MN
#1
Sports Fans
Based on number of sports teams, sports bars, sporting goods stores, and sports facilities.

Source: Sports & Fitness Magazine

100 seasons without a championship, and yet they come. The four major professional franchises have not won a major title since the Minnesota Twins won the 1991 World Series.

US Bank Stadium

Home to the Minnesota Vikings, it was built in 2016 and seats 66,200 at a cost of $1.2 billion. It is currently the state of the art in sports facilities.

Jim Gehrz ,©2016, Star Tribune

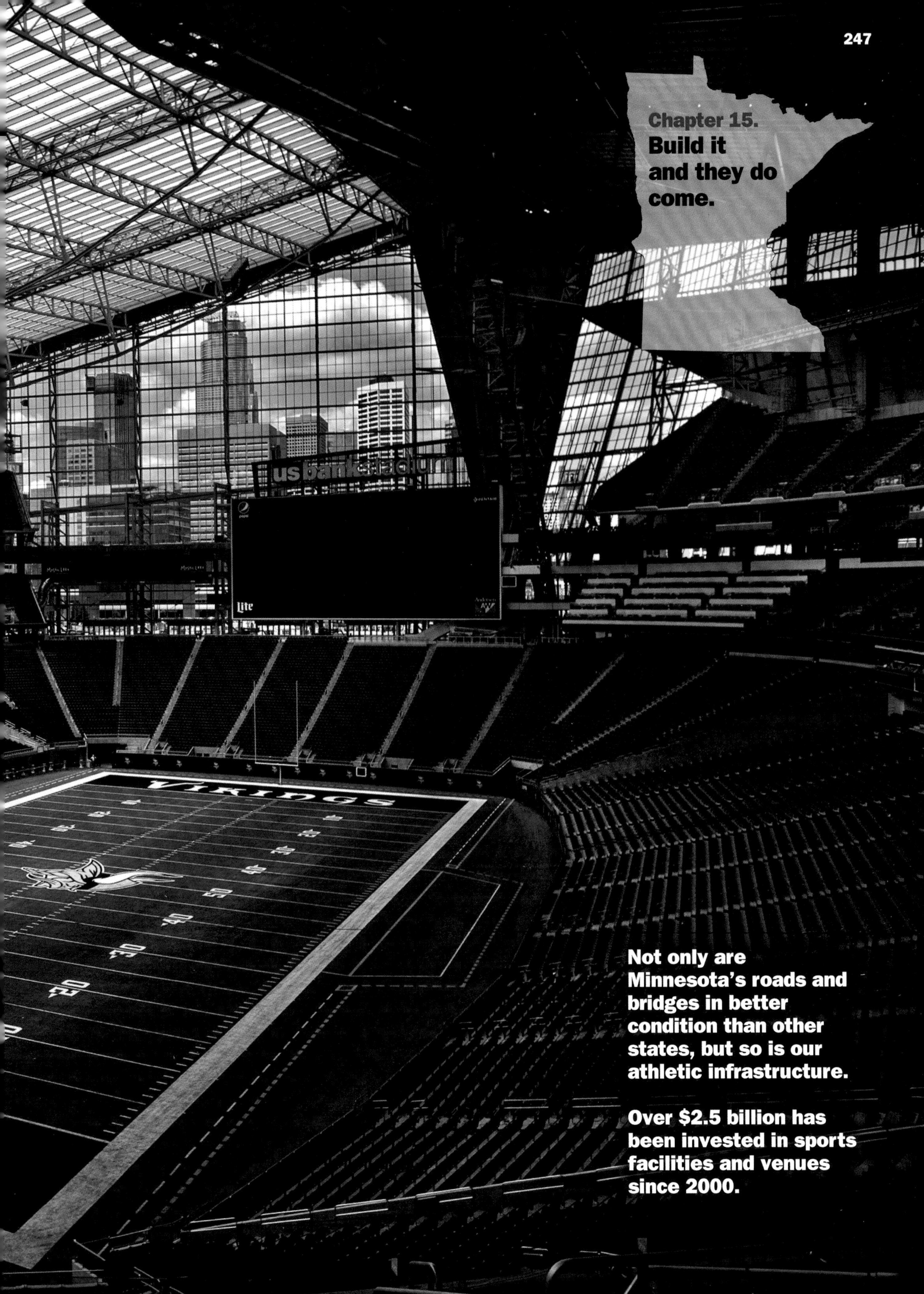

Chapter 15. Build it and they do come.

Not only are Minnesota's roads and bridges in better condition than other states, but so is our athletic infrastructure.

Over $2.5 billion has been invested in sports facilities and venues since 2000.

Target Field

Home to the Minnesota Twins, it was built in 2010 for $425 million and seats 40,000.

© Dan Anderson

CHS Field

The St. Paul Saints are the "other" professional baseball team in the Twin Cities. Built for $63 million in 2005, CHS Field seats 7,200. The picturesque park won first place in an international design contest.

Tom Wallace, © 2016, Star Tribune

The Xcel Center

Home to the Minnesota Wild hockey club, it opened in 2000. The center cost $170 million and seats 18,000 rabid fans.

Courtesy of Xcel Energy Center

© Minnesota Timberwolves

Target Center

Home to the Minnesota Timberwolves and the WNBA Lynx, it seats 20,000 and is currently being remodeled for $128 million.

University of Minnesota TCF Stadium

Built in 2012 for $335 million, it seats 52,525 and is about two miles from US Bank Stadium.

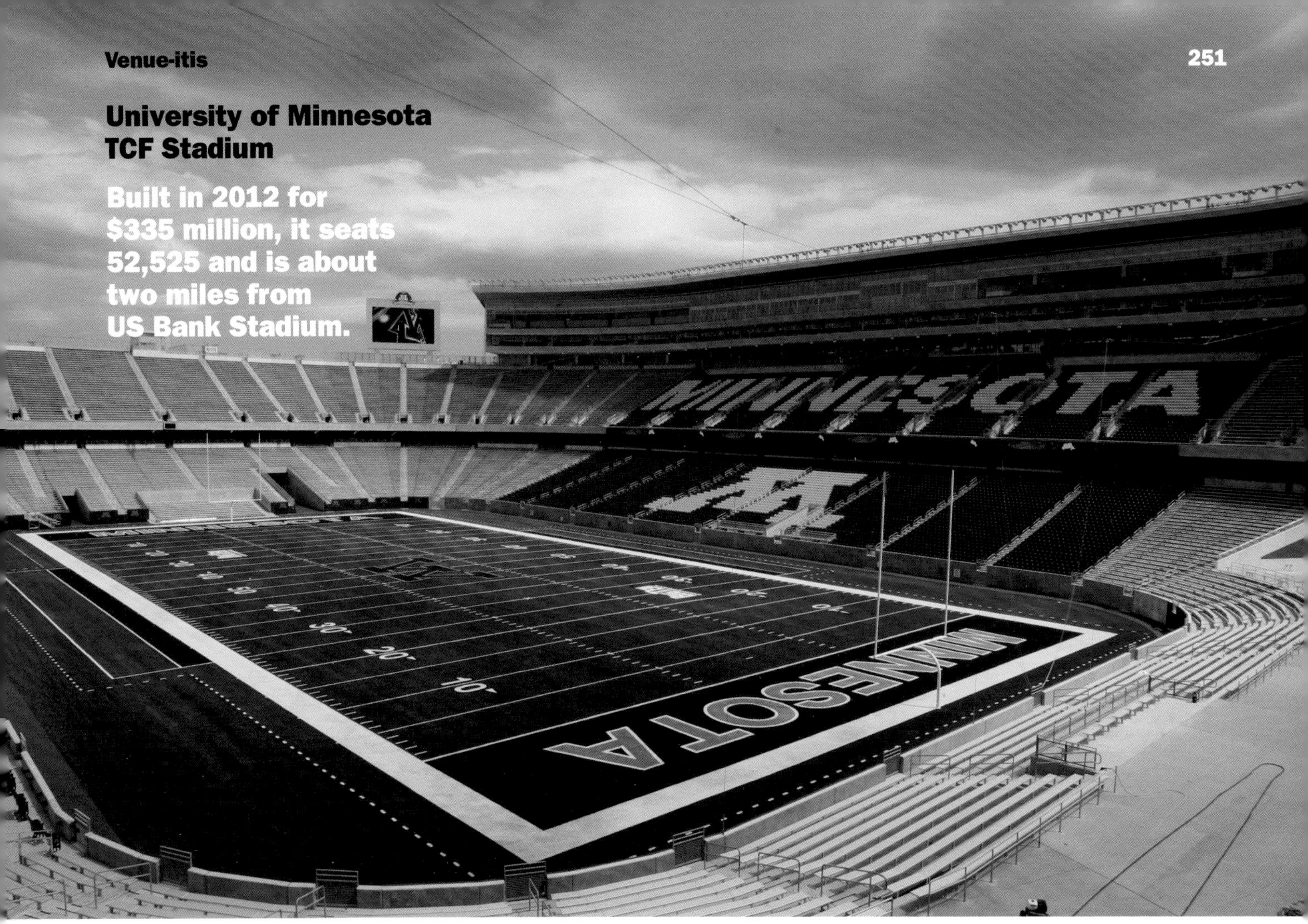

© *Nancy Kuehn, 2014* Mpls/St Paul Business Journal

The Twin Cities have not only the newest sporting palaces in the nation but also the most clustered. They are all within eight miles of each other. Most are just a few blocks apart.

Minnesota could easily be ready for the Olympic Games.

The north St. Paul suburb of Blaine is home to the largest sporting complex in the world: the National Sports Center (described in the recreation chapter).

© *irin-k / Shutterstock*

Minnesota United Field

Minnesota United FC, the new soccer franchise, will play in a new, yet-to-be-built stadium (architect's concept pictured below) costing $150 million and seating 20,000.

© Populous, Courtesy of Greater MSP

Minnesotans have always believed they have a great quality of life. Nevertheless, it's reassuring to read the many polls and surveys attesting to what we already know. The following pages contain just a few of the rankings and accolades Minnesota and the Twin Cities have recently enjoyed.

Chapter 16.
It's what it's all about.

Best Places to Grow Old

If you're old, or getting there, you'll like this. In spite of the weather, several different sources place Minnesota and the Twin Cities in the top five places to grow old. Educational opportunities, cultural life, parks, and sports attractions are important factors in this regard. Quality of health care and health facilities is the most important factor. Minnesota is home to seven of the top 100 hospitals in the nation.

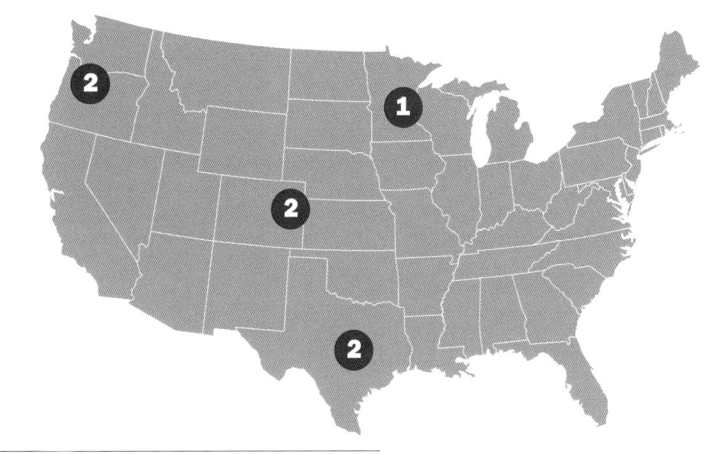

MN #1

Best Places to Live:

1. Twin Cities

2. Denver, Portland, & Austin; tied

Source: TravisNeighborWard.com

Rochester holds the record for the lowest ratio of median household income and lowest cost of living.

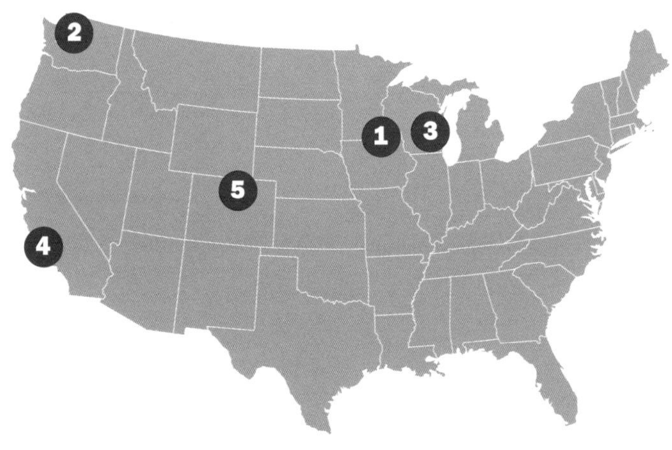

MN #1

Best Small Cities:

1. Rochester

2. Bellevue

3. Madison

4. Santa Barbara

5. Boulder

Source: livability 2015

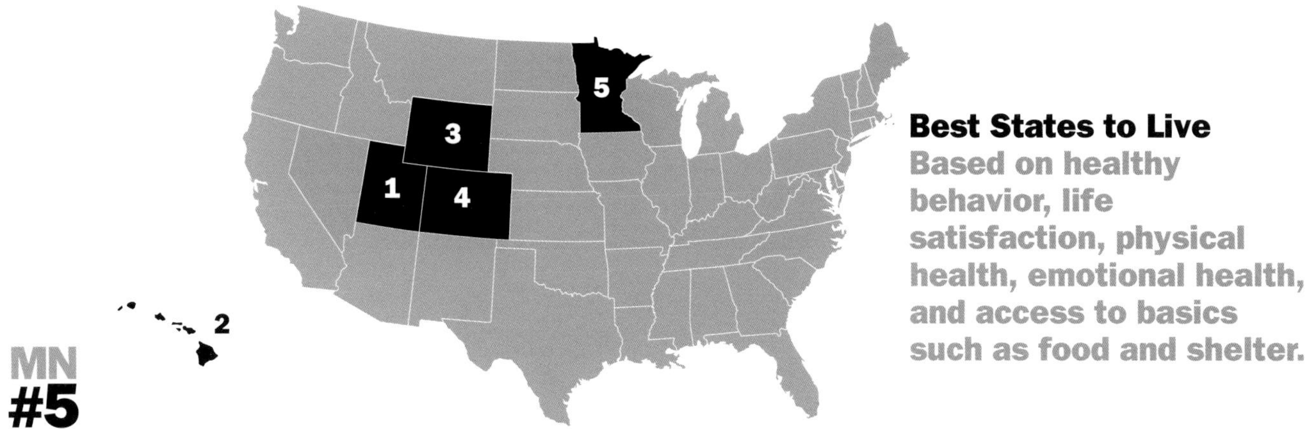

Best States to Live
Based on healthy behavior, life satisfaction, physical health, emotional health, and access to basics such as food and shelter.

Best States to Live In:

1. Utah
2. Hawaii
3. Wyoming
4. Colorado
5. **Minnesota**

Source: Forbes Magazine 2015

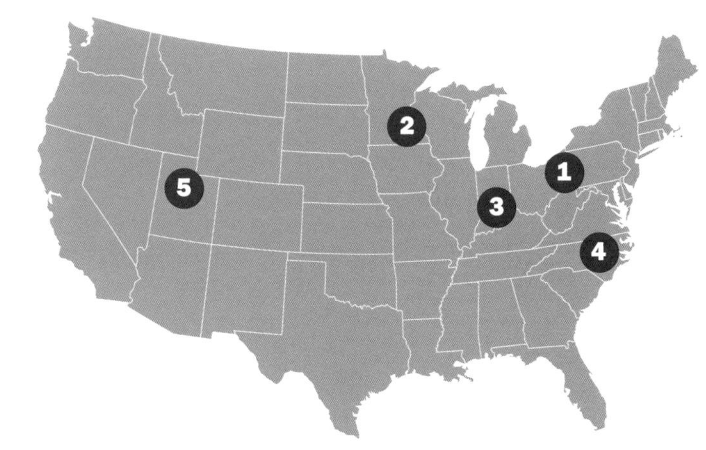

MN
#2

Best Downtowns:

1. Pittsburgh
2. **Minneapolis**
3. Indianapolis
4. Greenville
5. Salt Lake City

Source: livability 2015

A **$100,000** salary in the Twin Cities is worth:

a **$97,908** salary in Denver
a **$91,000** salary in Chicago
a **$75,263** salary in Seattle
a **$73,356** salary in Boston
a **$60,000** salary in San Francisco
a **$47,180** salary in New York City

Cost of Living

High median family income and low cost of living give the Twin Cities a financial advantage over other cities.

Source: Relocate America

MN #1

***Politico* Magazine Best States:**

1. **Minnesota**
2. New Hampshire
3. Vermont
4. Utah
5. Colorado

Based on criteria of annual income, employment percentage, poverty rates, home ownership, high school graduation rates, life expectancy, and deaths per 1,000 births.

© Shutterstock

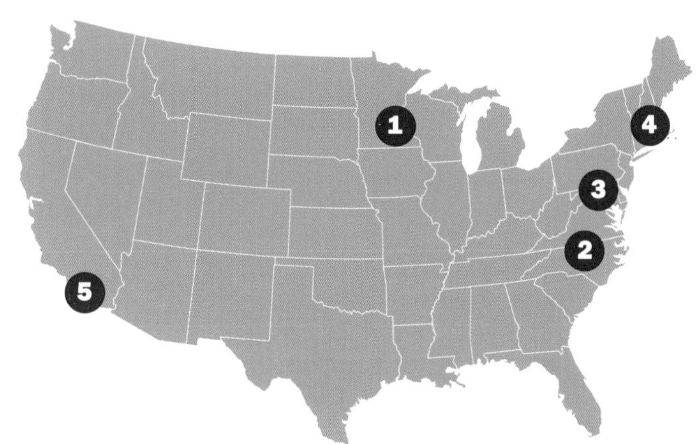

MN
#1

Least Stressful Cities to Live:

1. Twin Cities
2. Raleigh-Durham
3. Washington, DC
4. Boston
5. San Diego

Most Stressful Cities to Live:

1. Miami
2. New Orleans
3. Las Vegas
4. New York City
5. Portland

Source: Sperling's Best Places

The Twin Cities are #2 in access to the American Dream. The Opportunity Index is an annual composite measure at state and county levels of economics, education, and civic facts that expand opportunity.

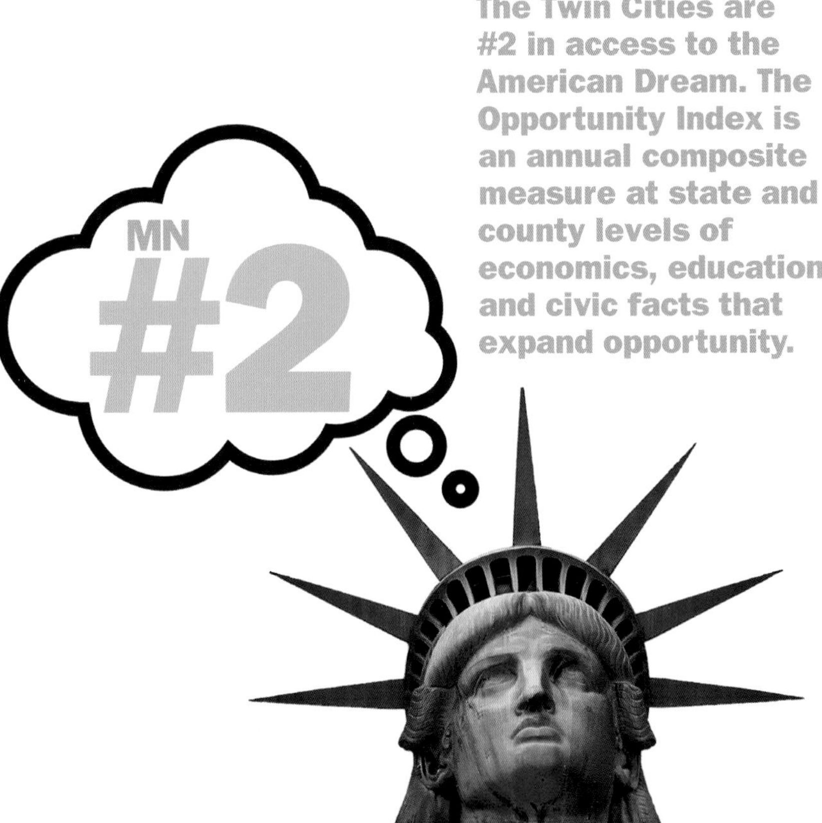

People often wonder how Twin Citians can afford to go to so many concerts, plays, and professional and college sporting events. Total spending annually could exceed $600 million. It is not uncommon for a ticket to cost $200 to $300.Where does the money come from? The Twin Cities rank fifth nationally in median household income.

We also enjoy a cost of living 20-25% lower than that of other cities in the top 10 for high household incomes. That gap between income and cost of living rewards the state with more disposable income—approximately $300 to $400 million more—for charitable contributions and entertainment expenses.

© Thomas Strand Studio LLC

I was born in a* City in a Park, *where 150 years ago lakes, the river, waterfalls, and woods were saved for everyone. Houses, streets, and corporate towers had to fit in between.

So I grew up in a* City in a Park, *where I swam in clean waters, biked for miles, learned to golf on a public course and play tennis on a public court, and played T-ball against kids from all over town because doesn't everyone have a public baseball diamond within six blocks of their house?

So there was never any question that I would raise my family in that* City in a Park, *where my kids swam in the same clean lakes, played on the same fields, sled down the same snowy hillsides—and I got to build a career that was only a short bike ride from my home and family.

So now I grow older in a* City in a Park, *where watching a blazing sunset across a lake with a skyline in the background, I see faces around me different than they were when I was little. There are still swimmers in bathing suits but also head-scarves, still hot dogs grilling but now with kimchi and harissa, still music playing but now with more hip-hop and world-beat—and I see an even better* City in a Park *where saving the best for everyone means* everyone *more than ever.

R. T. Rybak

president,
Minneapolis Foundation,
and former mayor of Minneapolis

© Joe Mamer Photography/Alamy

Duluth

The largest and furthest inland freshwater port is visited by more than 1,000 vessels from around the world each year. Iron ore pellets (taconite) and diversified commodities are shipped out through the Great Lakes and St. Lawrence Seaway. Minnesota's fifth-largest city is the gateway to the famous North Shore of Lake Superior, the Boundary Waters Canoe Area, and the Voyageurs National Wilderness Area. Thousands turn out to see the spectacular entry of the tall ships into Duluth Harbor.

Marine on St. Croix

One of the state's oldest and most quaint towns, this community of 600 residents nestles on the wild and scenic St. Croix River, only one hour from the city centers. Pictured is the General Store, formerly known as Ralph's Pretty Good Grocery.

© 2013 David A Parker Photography, LLC

© Gary Alan Nelson

Red Wing

Located 45 miles downriver from St. Paul, this beautiful city is home to not only famous pottery and boot companies, but also 17,000 folks who love music, beer, history, hiking, theater, antiques, golf, and river running. A historic hotel as well as scores of charming bed and breakfasts lure Twin Citians year-round.

© Doig Photography

© Matthew Winn

Grand Marais

Voted "America's Coolest Town" in 2015 by Budget Travel, its 1,500 residents live on the northern shore of Lake Superior. A large artist colony gathers in the summer along with water-loving tourists. The Naniboujou Lodge may have the most unusual interior of any restaurant in the nation and is a great place for lunch.

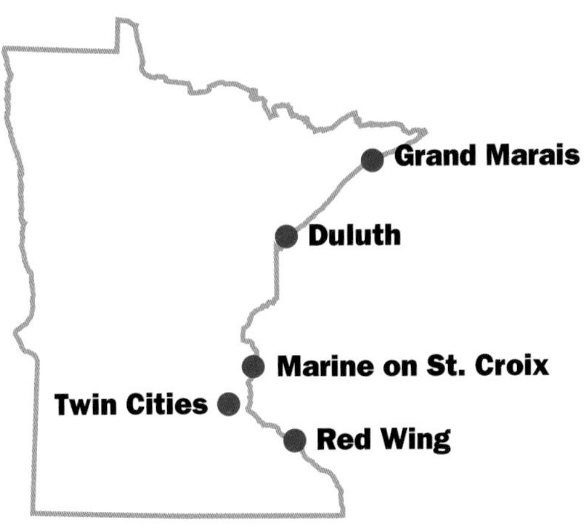

© Gina Kelly/Alamy

Tom Wallace,©2016,Star Tribune

Future Livability
An analysis of economics, weather, natural resources, population, and education ranks Minnesota at #2.

Source: Gallup.com/poll

© Ben's Mom

Meet Our Great-Grandson Benjamin
He was born in September 2016 and lives with his mom and dad in Phoenix, AZ. Chances are he will grow up in Phoenix, marry, and settle down in the city he is most familiar with.

Great-Grandpa (that's me) wonders what kind of environment Ben will be living in 30 years from now.

If climatologists are right, Phoenix will go from hot to very, very hot . . . possibly 10 to 20° hotter than today. Arizona will also go from dry to very, very dry. Water, which is in short supply now, will be incredibly precious in the future.

If Ben gets out of the heat and goes to the ocean, he will see flooding up close as many cities start to go underwater as sea levels rise.

San Francisco and Seattle will most likely have a "big one" in the next three decades, changing the contours of those cities.

Of course I think Ben should move to Minnesota. Our cold winters will continue to moderate. Our freshwater supply will be the envy of the nation.

Our economy should continue to be well balanced, so Ben should easily be able to find a job. And we will continue to invest in the arts and environment. Ben would be comfortable and safe in Minnesota.

Minnesota will be the state of the future. Ben should move to the State of the Future.

Amazing!

Lake Onamia

Lake Pepin

Lake Sanborn

Lake Washington

Lake Whitney

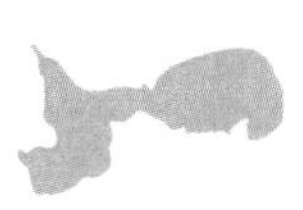

Lone Lake

Long Lake

Madison Lake

Marion Lake

Monson Lake

Mud Lake

North Goldsmith Lake

Ogechie Lake

Phelps Lake

Rabbit Lake

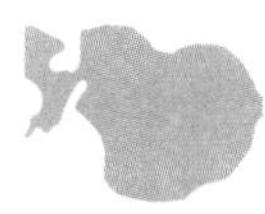

Renneberg Lake

Rice Lake

Ripple Lake

Savidge Lake

Schauer Lake

Schilling Lake

School Lake

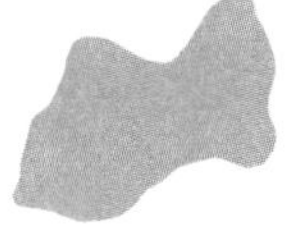

Section 12 Lake

Section 25 Lake

Severance Lake

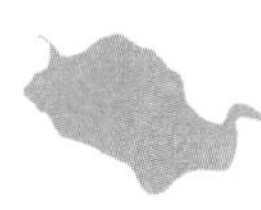

Shakopee Lake

Sheas Lake

Silver Lake

Spirit Lake

Sweetman Lake

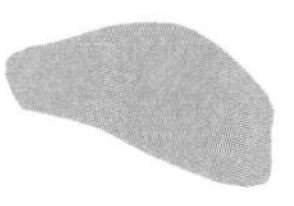

Tamarac Lake

Thomas Lake

Tietz Lake

Turtle Lake

Twenty Lake

Bakers Lake

Ballantyne Lake

Barber Lake

Black Bass Lake

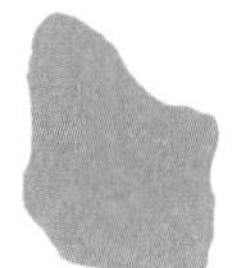

Borer Lake

Clarks Lake

Clear Lake

Curran Lake

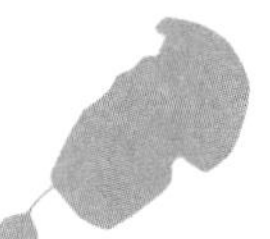

Dam Lake

Deer Lake

Dietz Lake

Dog Lake

Duban Lake

Duck Lake

Eagle Lake

Eagle (2) Lake

Eggert Lake

Fadden Lake

Farm Island Lake

George Lake

German Lake

Gilfillin Lake

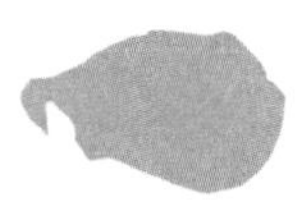

Goldsmith Lake

Graham Lake

Greenleaf Lake

Hanging Kettle Lake

Harkridge Lake

High Island Lake

Johnson Lake

Kings Lake

Lake Addie

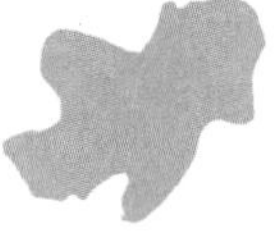

Lake Emily

Lake Henry

Lake Jefferson

Lake Mary